OUR COVER PICTURE: *The Forge*, a painting by Michael Herring. For further information on
Michael Herring's paintings, contact Image by Design: Tel & Fax: 0117 9863066

This quarterly *Country Origins* is published by Writers News Ltd, PO Box 4, Nairn IV12 4HU. Tel: 01667 454441. Fax: 01667 454401. Subscriptions are handled from the same address. The publisher is David St John Thomas.

Editorial contributions are welcome, but please study the magazine carefully or send a sae for Notes to Contributors. Contributions will not be acknowledged unless a stamped postcard is provided, and should be accompanied by a sae for their return if desired. Please write rather than phone on editorial matters. Note that the best articles are generally those with real information (and actual fact) and that suitable photographs (black and white or colour) greatly enhance the chances of publication.

It should be noted that we hold a large number of articles and cannot enter into correspondence regarding publication dates once material has been provisionally accepted. Neither the editor, Hilary Gray, nor the publishers can accept responsibility for material submitted.

Country Origins is published on the second Friday of March (spring), June (summer), September (autumn) and November (winter). It is distributed to the news trade by Diamond. Typesetting is by Writers News Ltd, PO Box 4, Nairn IV12 4HU, and colour repro by Posthouse Printing Ltd, Findhorn, Forres IV35 0TZ. The printer is Cradley Print Ltd, Chester Road, Cradley Heath, Warley, West Midlands B64 6AB. The advertising manager is Wendy Goodman, 94 Fore Street, Heavitree, Exeter EX1 2RS. Tel: 01392 213894 Fax: 01392 493228

COUNTRY TRADES
by Larry

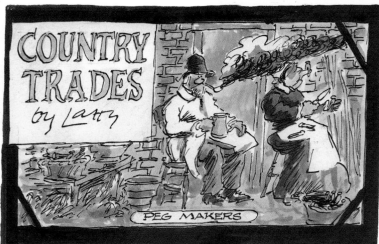

PEG MAKERS

THE CHARCOAL BURNER

THE OLD BOOTS AND SHOES SELLER

THE TIMBER FELLER

THE WHEELWRIGHT

THE BLACKSMITH

In Praise of Geese

David Watkins

'Now thrice welcome Christmas,
Which brings us good cheer,
Minc'd pies and plum-puddings
Good ale and strong beer,
With a pig, goose and capon,
The best that may be,
So well does the weather
And our stomachs agree'

THE above was a popular Christmas 'song' or carol of the Middle Ages, indicating that even then the goose was a traditional meat for the festive season. In modern times, we consume half a million of the birds each Christmas. The goose is still very much a luxury bird, though, since it sells at a much higher price in markets than the turkey.

Ancient Britons kept geese to be eaten and to be worshipped at the same time, since the bird was regarded as being sacred to Woden, the god of storm. Early kings of the realm collected their tributes, or taxes, in kind from their subjects. Geese were

A HAPPY NEW YEAR

TO YOU

demanded in this way, and in the 8th century the King of Wessex demanded from one village no less than 300 loaves of bread, ten sheep and fifty geese.

Such geese were always welcome at Christmas time when royal dinners would begin at midday and last for some eight or nine hours. Every farm and cottage in Britain once had its own flock of geese. These birds had a distinct advantage over all other types of poultry since their feed costs were low due to their grazing habits. Though they vary considerably in size and quality, some ganders can weigh up to 20lb and geese up to 17lb.

The popularity of geese as Christmas fare increased as time went by, and poorer families managed to secure a goose for themselves to celebrate Christmas.

In 1284, Edward I granted a charter to Nottingham to hold an annual

FOR XMAS DAY IN THE MORNING

THE XMAS GEESE.

Goose Fair, and during the following years it was estimated that no less than 20,000 geese were offered for sale during the three weeks that the Fair lasted each year. Yet another popular Goose Fair was established at Tavistock in Devon to supply the local people with traditional meat for Christmas.

At about this time, the swan also became popular Christmas meat amongst the nobility, but the goose was never ousted from the table. In 1274, the price of a swan was no less than three shillings while the price of a goose remained at the low price of five pence.

The goose, of course, was the grey lag which bred in great numbers in the fens of eastern England, and while large numbers of these were killed for eating every year, many were left unmolested to breed yet again. However, when the fens were

Greetings.

May every joy this
Christmastide
Your heart desires appear,
And health and happiness
provide
True blessings through
the year.

drained, the bird did not breed there any longer and as its numbers were reduced it became profitable to keep tame ones. Soon, huge flocks were being reared, in Lincolnshire in particular.

The big cities were excellent markets for the sale of geese around Christmas time, and thousands were traditionally sold at Smithfield.

Huge armies of geese were driven by farmers from all over the country especially from Norfolk, Suffolk and Wales to London, often more than a thousand strong, and this arduous journey had to be undertaken many weeks prior to Christmas since the birds were such slow travellers, covering some eight to ten miles every day. Before commencing the journey, however, they were firstly driven through tar and then through sand in order to give protection to their feet. Many place names testify to the gatherings of geese and to their long journeys. Gosford in Devonshire is derived from two words 'Goose Ford' and Gosport in Hampshire means a 'market place where geese were sold'. Daniel Defoe, the famous author of *Robinson Crusoe*, described how he had witnessed a flock of no less than 2,000 geese travelling to London from various parts of the country. The goose was not only popular for its meat. Geese were plucked as often as five times a year in order to collect their down and feathers for pillows and bed mattresses. In addition, their feathers were also carefully preserved to be used as quills for writing until well past the middle of the 19th century. In Victorian times, the goose was very much in favour

everywhere, and in the immortal *Christmas Carol* by Charles Dickens we read of a family enjoying a goose meal at Christmas time especially since costlier meat could not be afforded. Verses in praise of the goose also appeared in Mrs Beeton's Christmas Annual of 1868 where its virtues are lauded highly as a meat over other types of traditional meat:

'*The turkey is good, and the capon's
    fine,
The partridge is quite to my taste;
Off a couple of fowls I sometimes dine,
Or pigeons baked in a paste;
But not one of those could me induce
To forsake my favourite fat roast goose*

*Stuff her with onion, mix with sage,
Nicely baste and carefully roast,
Serve with brown gravy and apple
    sauce
And let me dine as a guest or a host;
Let me be both, it will better suit me,
For a goose and I are good company*'

High praise indeed for the humble goose whose popularity stretches back through the centuries in the history of this country.

Happy New Year

On New Year's morning in Herefordshire a plaited crown of prickly blackthorn was held by the fire until it was scorched. The remains were then hung up with the mistletoe to be kept as a Luckbringer. – *Ann Redmayne*

A right, merry Christmas

With best wishes for a happy Christmas.

Ahead of Steam

THE ALLURE OF STEAM FAIRS AND STEAM RALLIES

Text and pictures by John Hannavy

WHAT is it about that intoxicating mixture of hot oil, and coal smoke, which carries it so far on the wind? You can smell it long before you can see it, be it a preserved steam railway

Changing places at the St Agnes Steam Rally in August, Garrett No 30959, built in 1912, prepares for the show ring which Aveling & Porter No 9197, built 1920, has just left.

recreating the golden era of railway transport, or one of the many annual steam fairs and rallies which evoke strong memories of steam rollers rolling hot tar on country roads, or of traction engines powering a profusion of farmyard and woodyard tools in days gone by.

When Aveling & Porter, of Rochester in Kent, modified an early

steam engine which required to be horse-drawn to wherever its power was needed, into the first self-powered engine in the late 1850s, they can hardly have foreseen the impact their experiment was destined to have on rural Britain.

Even less likely is it that they could have foreseen that their design for an industrial workhorse would become, over a century and a quarter later, a

Burrell 'Forrester' showman's engine seen at a rally in Lancashire

magnet for tens of thousands of tourists across the British Isles.

These massive and powerful machines – some horse-drawn, most self-powered were built in their many thousands over a period of a little over a century – the first in the 1840s. The first self-powered machine

Opposite 'Little Billie', a 7.5 ton Garrett engine from 191, was owned by several generations of the Cole family, famous showmen from Gloucestershire. It is seen here at the 1996 West of England Steam Engine Society Rally.

rolled off the production line before 1860, and the last — a steam-powered road roller — left the Vickers Armstrong factory on Tyneside in 1950.

Despite the fact that almost one hundred companies were engaged at one time or another in the construction of traction engines, road roller and steam-powered lorries, the market was dominated by just a few well known names. Amongst them

are the names of John Fowler of Leeds, Aveling & Porter of Rochester, Kent, Charles Burrell of Thetford, Richard Garrett of Leiston, Suffolk, and Joseph Foden of Sandbach, Cheshire, perhaps best remembered for steam-powered lorries, and a name still proudly carried by today's huge juggernauts.

Like steam locomotives when diesel and electric was in the ascendancy, traction engines and road rollers were destroyed with almost wilful speed as petrol and diesel-

'Betsy', seen here at a steam fair in the East Lancashire Railway, is owned by world-famous steeplejack, Fred Dibnah. (Also see page 16).

'Betsy', seen here at a steam fair in the East Lancashire Railway, is owned by world-famous steeplejack, Fred Dibnah. (Also see page 15).

Steam was *the* power source for so many years, and was applied to powering just about everything from the humble monolithic road roller to the delicate and tuneful fairground organ. And self-powered steam engines worked every sort of farmyard and field tool – ploughing, harrowing, lifting, sawing, pumping and draining. On the road, huge steam engines pulled 'road trains' across Britain – only they had the power and the endurance to draw huge loads for long distances.

The sheer size of some of the engines is awesome – and thankfully steam rallies and fairs afford the opportunity to get up close enough to appreciate that size. While the general purpose engines which worked farmyard equipment were large by most standards, those which worked huge ploughing rigs, or drew the road trains, were truly massive.

In sharp contrast to the drab working garb of the industrial and agricultural engines, the showman's engines were painted in lively bright colours, kept meticulously clean, and as a result, were widely admired.

They had two purposes – first they were the workhorses which draw fairground rides and caravans around the country, and secondly, with their steam-powered generators, they were the power source which lit the brightly coloured fair-

powered machinery usurped their role both on the road and in the field. However, hundreds survived the cutter's torch – often by default rather than design – and have today been lovingly restored back to full operating standards.

Collecting and preserving traction engines is now more popular than ever before, guaranteeing that there will be a wide range of fascinating old machines, all in working order, to steam their way across the fairgrounds of Britain.

The term 'traction engine' embraces a wide range of machines – with as wide a range of functions.

Opposite 'Billy' is believed to be the oldest working example of a general purpose steam engine. Built by Burrell's of Thetford in 1895 for an Ayrshire farmer who cancelled the order, this engine spent its working life in the fields of Suffolk.

Welcome to the winter issue which starts the third year of *Country Origins*. And thanks for all your comments and of course, support. Could I make these points?

1. Our nostalgic calendar is now available. A nostalgic country scene for each month of the year (plus more), will give endless pleasure during 1998 and represents marvellous value for money. See page 146.

2. A year's subscription (four issues) plus the calendar makes a wonderful gift guaranteed to give year-round please. (And do not forget those overseas relatives and friends who might be especially pleased to have it.) See card between pages 114-115.

3. Readership is growing nicely but of course many have not discovered us. Your personal introduction through our Introduce a Friend scheme will be most appreciated. See card between pages 114-115.

4. You nearly all think we give excellent value for money. Do remember that postal subscriptions are especially beneficial (to you as well as us) and support us this way if you possibly can. See card between pages 114-115.

5. We hope shortly to publish an index of our first eight issues. Look for further announcement.

LIKE ALL NEWISH MAGAZINES
WE NEED ALL THE HELP YOU CAN GIVE!

David St John Thomas

ground rides, so much a part of country fairs throughout late 19th and early 20th century Britain. Many engines were built specially for fairground use, while others were converted from more mundane purposes into these wonderfully ostentatious extravaganzas of colour and polished brass work. Yet beneath the twisted

06007 *Opposite* **No 11111 'City of Hull' was one of a large number of road locomotives built by John Fowler of Leeds – this one in 1910. Like so many of today's working traction engines, it has been completely rebuilt.**

metalwork, and polished stars and bright paintwork, there was a versatile immensely powerful and thoroughly reliable steam engine. It had to be – for during fairs it was constantly working to keep the showground lit and alive, and the rides operational. Between fairs, these engines pulled the dismantled rides and roundabouts and, at the end of an often long train of vehicles, the showman's caravan containing his living quarters.

Showman's engines, typically, have full-length canopies over them, partly for show, and partly to keep the worst of the weather off the generating equipment.

Today's steam fairs offer a rich mixture of all engine types, including steam lorries, military engines, showman's engines, and farm equipment.

At the West of England Traction Engine Rally held in St Agnes, Cornwall, each August – typical of over a hundred such fairs throughout the country – these giants parade around the ring, while others stand in line, gently simmering awaiting their turn. Rows of stationary engines, purring and whirring, demonstrate their former roles, pumping water, sawing timber and a host of other tasks.

Across the huge show ground, massive traction engines power threshing machines and baling machines, while others power cranes and huge circular saws allowing their owners to reduce trees to fence-posts and planks of rough hewn weatherboarding. The air is thick with that wonderful smell, and that evocative sound. For the photographers amongst us, our view is a rich mixture of shapes and colours, punctuated by plumes of pure white steam against the deep blue of a summer sky.

The popularity of these events grows annually. Magazines like *Old Glory* celebrate the history and preservation of the steam engine, as well a publicising many of the steam fairs and rallies held across the country. Books on steam traction are growing in number, and one publisher, Shire Publications, has two

06003 'Hero" built by McLaren in 1918, worked as a ploughing engine – the drum of steel hawsers can be seen under the boiler. This huge 22 ton engine is believed to be the sole survivor of its type.

interesting and inexpensive books currently in their lists. *Traction Engines* and *Farming with Steam*, both by Harold Bonnett, cost £2.25 and £4.99 respectively.

You don't have to wait for the summer to see these magnificent engines. There is a small but important collection at Levens Hall in Cumbria, several preserved examples at the Beamish Open Air Museum in Northumberland, the Charles Burrell Collection in Thetford in Norfolk, and examples in many other farming and transport museums throughout the country. They are much more impressive, though, when they are on the move!

HOW DID THEY DO THAT?
Preserve food

WE rely on our freezers and fridges, have rapid transportation to get food quickly to the shops we use, and yet keeping food in good condition especially in summer can still present a challenge, so how was it possible for food such as grapes to have been available out of season, and how were other foods preserved?

Go back in time and we find that country folk lived largely on meal and milled grain in the form of porridge or bread as the main constituent of each meal. Dairy products, eggs, an occasional chicken at the end of its laying time and perhaps a pig fattened for special times of the year would brighten up the tedious menu occasionally, as would berries and fruit in summer.

Vegetables could survive if left in the ground, or in earth clams, and food could be stored for a period in caves of deep earth-covered caverns, where the temperature was nearly stable throughout the year. Some larger houses built ice houses, a stone lined hole in the ground into which ice or snow was pushed and which kept cold for long periods. Some large houses including some in towns have several levels of cellars including a low stone lined arched one that is as cool throughout the year as a cave.

Fruit and to a limited degree meat could be dried and stored although the place where it was stored had to be kept very dry. Pickling and fermenting in various forms allowed

Very early refrigerator open and closed

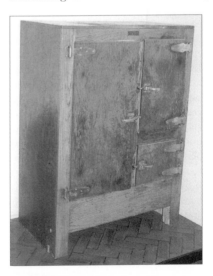

A second early refrigerator

fruit and some other items to be kept, as did salting and smoking, the principle objective of any means of storage being to eliminate or reduce the growth of micro organisms, enzyme action and oxidation. David Livingstone, the missionary and explorer, wrote from Zambesesi in 1859 to Frederick Ketch of London, to say how well the hams he had been supplied with had kept and wrote two years later to say that two that he had kept were still in their original condition. While some like Ketch had perfected the process, others were less reliable.

Animals years ago were taken in herds to where they were to be killed and eaten so we read of cattle drives from Wales to London and Wiltshire pigs originally being taken but later cured in Wiltshire and the preserved

meats coming from the west country and as requirements grew also from Ireland. Milk was more difficult to transport and the UK dairy industry not as large or organised, so much of the dairy produce used in the cities such as London was imported from the continent. Conversion of some farms from mixed to dairy farms started in the late 1860s or 1870s and over the next thirty years as around a third of the workforce left the land, six million acres were added to the permanent pasture. The first cheese factory in the UK opened in 1871, and the first dairy company was set up by a London milk dealer in 1871 in the west country, and had six collecting depots by 1889. In 1904 *Country Life* carried an article about the development of preserved milk, referred to as aerated or pasteurised, and doubting if it had any use other than for ships and other long journeys. However, it acknowledged the public fear of illness from milk produced under poor conditions.

There were also many skills now largely forgotten such as hanging up bunches of grapes with their stems dipped in small glass flasks containing a mixture including sugar, water and charcoal, and in this form the grapes lasted for many months. Likewise some other early precautions have been until recently overlooked but after food poisoning rediscovered, such as the distinction between the grocer who sold cooked meats and the butcher who sold raw meats. The original fear was of the uncooked meat being contaminated by the salt and smoked surface of the preserved meat than the other way around. Eggs were stock piled when in supply and sold when prices rose due to shortages. To keep eggs from going bad the shells had to be protected from the air by rubbing them in butter, lard or gum water, and then standing them with the small end through a perforated card, or packed in dry ash or lime.

Canning came about in the early 19th century and freezing early in the 20th century. Initially freezing was slow and large crystals formed turning all frozen foods to a stodge, but once quick freezing was discovered by Clarence Birdseye in 1924 and freezers had freezing compartments the crystal size was reduced and food was no longer destroyed to the same degree.

While early diets were of the kind some people would still recommend today, many of the foods we know today have been relatively recent inventions. In 1895 Heinz produced their first batch of tins of baked beans, which up to WW2 also contained a piece of pork, but due to the war shortages was then dropped. Baked beans were first manufactured in the UK in 1928. Suet making started in 1893 by Atora of Hereford and for many years up to the 1940s Atora suet was delivered to the shops in colourful wagons pulled by six pairs of Hereford bullocks, the wagons later being sold to Chipperfield's Circus. Tinned cream from Ambrosia came about in 1933, and Ambrosia Rice Pudding in 1937. Walls were manufacturing pies when refrigeration was in its infancy but found it difficult to sell pies at some points of the year as people believed

that pork should not be eaten in the months that did not have an R in it, the four warmer months of the year. When Walls came up with their ice cream, their then customers – butchers and fishmongers – saw no future in it and they resorted to buying a tricycle to get rid of the first batch of ice cream on 6 July 1922, which grew into a fleet of 8,500 tricycles in 1939. Smiths crisps started in 1921, and until 1939 was on a manual basis with a large tank of ground nut oil used to cook each batch.

A Gift for the Poor

This ancient lock-up in the west country village of Castle Gary was built in 1779 with money bequeathed for 'Gifts to the poor of the Parish'. It is not recorded what the poor of the Parish thought of this 'gift' but it is known that as late as 1785 it was used to incarcerate children caught playing truant from school or playing ball on Sundays. – *R. Dixon*

Travelling the West Country in the 1950's

David St John Thomas

ONE of the joys of reporting the West Country in the 1950s was the travelling around. In those days it was not so much a region as a series of towns and districts of great individuality loosely connected by often infrequent trains, buses and of course ferries.

Distances were far longer than most people realised, and with not a single mile of dual carriageway either in Cornwall or the administrative county of Devon journey times could be considerable. If two trains left Paddington and Penzance at the same time they passed near Dawlish Warren.

Just about everywhere seemed the wrong starting point, for most places of importance were on the coast or near the head of estuaries, and journeys of any distance meant going east or west against the grain of the terrain. The main railways managed a few really fast trains, but they were mostly in the middle of the day for holiday folk travelling to the resorts. Thus the Cornish Riviera Express ran non-stop to Plymouth, which it did in a highly-creditable four hours, and then only stopped at Par, Truro, Gwinear Road and St Erth before reaching Penzance. All the intermediate stops were junctions for branch lines to the resorts, with only Truro being significant in its own right. To reach more workaday places like St Austell, and the twin mining centres of Redruth and Camborne, meant taking a slower service. Only once was this reporter able to take afternoon tea on the prestige train from Plymouth to Penzance, in readiness for the boat to the Scilly Isles the next day.

Our base at Plymouth was a particularly bad starting point for regional journeys. Getting to

Cornwall involved a lengthy diversion via what was then the first bridge over the Tamar at Gunnislake, or at busy times seemingly endless wait for the Saltash or Torpoint Ferry. Even on morning visits to the coast not far into Cornwall you could spend four-fifths of your time in the queue for the Torpoint Ferry. Delays of two and a half hours were the norm.

In the other direction, to Exeter, one faced what was claimed to be the longest lane in England: the narrow, winding A38 where at busy times overtaking opportunities were truly minimal. Today it takes well under an hour to Exeter; then two and a half hours of tiring driving was by no means unusual, and that before there was a break-down or accident.

There were, however, several pleasant consequences. One was that, out of the office, one was very much one's own person. Only when you came to telephone 'the story', itself a hazardous enough business on the archaic telecommunications systems, were you back under command. Against the time scale, short explorations on the side seemed a small imposition on the employer who was general served well, certainly in terms of sheer hours spent on the job. And since so few people travelled throughout the region, welcomes were often warm and it was possible unofficially to trade one piece of information with another.

Another benefit was the amount one could earn in car allowances. Even in 1951, it was an old sixpence a mile, outside the city of Plymouth where bus was supposed to be obligatory even if the service had closed

down for the night. A journey of twenty miles each way therefore earned a pound, or over a fifth of take-home salary after normal deductions. Frequently car allowances were greater than salary. The faithful 1938 Morris Eight, whose business trips took the mileage from 70,000 to 140,000 before a replacement was finally afforded, suffered Big End and most other troubles, and repair bills were a problem. But still jobs in the country paid handsomely... especially if there were a passenger or two. Though the Harmsworth people were not noted for generosity, it was 6d per passenger, and one could get away with that even if the passenger could perfectly well have travelled most of the way by train.

The really profitable journeys were to events calling for a contingent of head office reporters to supplement the local ones. In the last days that the Devon County and Royal Cornwall, and even the Bath & West and the Royal shows moved around their respective territories, encouraging or even bribing others to share the car trip (when would one start, where would each person sit, would meals be at the driver's expense?) was eminently worth while. Four to South Molton or Redruth, with additional journeys ferrying people to and from the show and town or hotel, offered a veritable fortune.

The other highly desirable consequence of long journey times for the impecunious single reporter was the need to spend nights away. In those days a night in just about any hotel in any strange town was a treat. Though the standard lunch allowance was

Travel from Plymouth might mean taking a push-pull auto-car train across the royal Albert Bridge to Saltash, or a slow-moving fifteen-coach double-headed 'express' down the main line to a variety of destinations including Penzance where the Cornishman train from Wolverhampton shown in this 1959 photograph is heading.

mean, overnight it was possible to have the tab picked up at any reasonable hotel. And when this one became the holiday reporter, there was even a need to test the luxury end of the market.

Such nights away might be a treat by the standards of those days, and enjoyable it often was in the company of the brigade of commercial travellers and meeting with the local reporter. Standards of food, service and hygiene were however awful: even at Cornwall's only four-star hotel, a request for ice in the water was met by removing some from under wine bottles. Portions were mean, meat often tough, puddings as unimaginative and unfilling as only half a dozen stewed plums in lumpy custard can be. Fruit juices were frequently extra on top of forfeiting soup, choice minimal so that at some breakfasts it had to be a kipper. Many single rooms were unimproved since the war and, at places where everyone ate together at the same time, queues for the toilets infuriating. One vast hotel, late paying its phone bill, had its phones ripped out other than one in reception (which had presumably been paid for) not available to guests.

Fond memories of the Metropole at Padstow as the first to offer a four-course dinner with fish and meat, and of an earlier trip to Padstow which brought the joy of buying the first off-the-ration small packet of biscuits at a refreshment room at Bodmin Road, the junction station. A tin of mum's rock cakes replenished fortnightly was a guarded treasure on such trips.

The best and worst of meals and rooms were at bed and breakfast places. One landlady said that clean sheets were possible if somehow one could dry them oneself in a room without fire. Radiators were rare even in fully-fledged hotels. But some ladies prided themselves on their breakfasts, and most were fine if you did not wince at the occasional maggot in the bacon, or at an egg slightly past its prime. You also had to accept an excess of grease and burnt toast made an hour ago. Just filling oneself up was object enough.

Nights were sometimes punctuated by drunks, including occasionally one of our own, on the rampage, or vociferous quarrels, or by smoke caused by someone smoking in bed rudely woken up with a bucket of water to douse him and fire. Drink was high up the priority list for most, and great was the upset when a party of us were booked into a temperance hotel at Exeter. We were actually on our way to the Royal Show at Newton Abbot but, because the office had left booking late and everywhere locally was full, they put us at Exeter, being closer to Newton in the morning than Plymouth. It was more than one boozy reporter could take to be put in a temperance hotel at all, but when it was clear that he would have to share a room with the writer, and there was only a double bed at that, all hell and bad language broke out. Eventually to great mutual relief and simply to prevent everyone in the temperance establishment hearing such profanity, the proprietor and wife gave up their own room.

Memories are colourful, but also long so far as food is concerned, and West Country tourism suffered grievously by the first generation of post-war visitors ever after recalling poor treatment. Today's young travellers have no notion of how welcome another swede used to be simply to fill oneself up. Many speak nostalgically about 1950s holidays but have never returned West since.

Hard Winters

WHEN water supplies froze, it was children's work to fill the copper with snow on wash days. As ten buckets of snow melted to 2ins of water, it took most of the morning to produce enough for the weekly wash and rinse. Then every drop was recycled, heaved to barrels for flushing cisterns and washing floors during the rest of the week. – *Hilary Lloyd*

REFLECTIONS

Yesterday's Country People

Bill Sharpe, village barber

IN true Happy Families tradition found in so many villages, Mr Smith ran the forge, Mrs Bone worked at the butcher's assisted by Mrs Greentree, who would have been more appropriately placed in the greengrocer's next door if that were not already occupied by Mrs Andrews who was, no doubt, an aid to regular habits and good digestion. It will, therefore, be no surprise to learn that the barber was Mr Sharpe.

The barber's was only open on Wednesdays and Saturdays when Bill Sharpe would arrive on the ten o'clock bus from his home in a nearby market town. He carried the tools of his trade in a squat and battered wooden box with suitcase clips and handle. Like many barbers, Bill's own hair was rather sparse apart from the unruly tufts which sprouted from his ears.

Bill rented the little lock-up shop which had previously been the saddlers although a faded turn of the century photograph shows a small sign beside the door announcing that he was a 'Hair Cutter' as well.

It was rather bare inside and almost lavatorially painted blue below and cream above a red dado line. The ill-fitting linoleum bore holes worn in places where feet no longer trod and suggested that it had already seen active service elsewhere. Waiting customers were provided with a couple of comfortable old bus seats upholstered in a moth-eaten moquette with a broad leather border and nickel plated grab handles. For entertainment there was a selection of dog-eared sporting magazines and tattered comics and an elderly fretwork fronted wireless crackled to itself from a corner shelf. It would occasionally become quite distinct as Bill moved closer in the course of his gyrations around his current client. His hearing aid would somehow excite the airwaves and awaken the wireless before whistling back in response.

The wooden barber chair had an adjustable neck rest while seating height was graduated according to the customer's stature by either sitting on the tool box or on a short board resting on the chair arms. The chair faced a once grand and spindle shelved overmantel mirror now garishly painted blue and suspended above a large sink mounted on cast iron brackets with ornamental acanthus leaf scrollwork which must have had a previous existence supporting a heavy lavatory cistern. The pair of proud upright taps were not plumbed in and hot water came from a brown enamel electric kettle and cold from a floral patterned washstand jug. Waste water trickled through the hair-bunged plughole into a disreputable looking chipped white enamel slop pail. At the end of each day Bill would jettison the contents into a gutter outside.

A glazed cabinet to the left of the mirror held a few faded cards of combs, green packets of 'Seven O'clock' razor blades and the blue Gillettes each with the face of moustached King C Gillette sneering out above his signature trade mark. There were bottles of 'Harlene – for the hair' and some ladies' requisites including 'New curl size Kirbigrips – ideal for small curls' and packets of hairnets 'handmade from quality sterilised human hair', not collected from Bill's plughole, one hoped!

The actual haircutting process followed a precise series of operations by which one could predict the waiting time for your turn in the chair. Once you were seated and wrapped about the shoulders in a bit of sheet, Bill would clamp you by the shoulders and ask 'Now?'. This was your cue to request 'Just a trim, please' or, if you were really brave, 'Short back and sides, please'. Bill's poor hearing had to be borne in mind when placing the order. Best results were accomplished by clear diction right into his face, mumblers were rarely satisfied...

The snipping, with scissors and comb, began at a fairly frenzied pace reminiscent of Bernard Miles' Hertfordshire barber who 'had two prices so's you could either have it cut or notched. Only difference was when he was notching he went a lot faster and he wasn't so careful...'

Rudimentary conversation took place, Wednesdays usually involved the weather – 'They give it wet for the weekend, then?' or 'Nice to have it dry again, ent it?', whereas Saturdays tended to be more sport orientated with special speculation as to how 'Pompey' would get on that day.

After the snipping came the clipping, the hand operated clippers squeaking as they crept up the neck like a metallic rabbit. Any spots were greedily devoured by the merciless nibblings and one could not help wondering about other necks and

The saddler's shop with 'hair cutter' just visible to left of doorway

other spots through which those little teeth had sliced before you!

Clipping finished and the ordeal was almost over, well almost, because it was time for the cut-throat razor. Two of them lay open on a spindle shelf glinting menacingly at their reflections in the mirror while the long leather tongue of the strop lolled thirstily towards the sink. Young imaginations conjured up Sweeney Todd and his pies!

With a few deft strokes your side-boards were straight and Bill would again clamp his hands on your shoulders with a 'Now – anythin' on?'. This meant which hairdressing, if any, did you require? The choice was a few squirts of a substance which smelled like syrup of figs and dried like shellac or a dollop of runny cream which oozed from a dispenser and left the head feeling stickily refrigerated for the rest of the day.

Whether you chose a squirt, a dollop or nothing at all the final stage was always a fairly harsh brushing alternated with some graceful 'hand-moulding'. The oblong two-handled mirror was flashed, for your approval, behind the neck giving a brief glimpse of the beheaded spots. Then, with a hey presto gesture, the sheet was whipped away, the dusting brush flicked across your collar, you paid up and were free... – *Michael Wall*

Student laddie

IN northern Scotland, June's dawn was already a memory when Viewfield's morning milking started at 4am. Ian Grant, the farmer, was well satisfied with Hector, his cattleman, brisk and efficient, never once missing a minute, but the new student laddie... Oh, he had a lot to learn. Away from home for the first time, often in a daze after the night before, head ringing after tackety boot dances in the village hall or pleasantly dreamy after an evening's courting along the deserted Bear's Head beach, there were occasions when his bed was never warmed. He would just about cope till the cows were out to pasture and then he collapsed, dead to the world till the afternoon shift at two.

Winter was another matter. Faced with over a hundred cattle quartered indoors, forty of them milkers, all bellowing for specialised feeding and mucking out – the laddie's jobs – and a horse-drawn lorry-load of sloshing churns to get to Elgin Creamery however treacherous the weather, Mr Grant vowed yet again that this time next year would, *really* would, see him sold up and settled in South America, *Central* South America!

Viewfield from the air in October 1959. There are still stacks in the cornyard. Among the trees on the left, on the north side of the hill is hidden an ice-house. North is approximately top left corner from the house.

By then, though, the laddie was learning. Except for the Young Farmers' annual 'do', he now knew better than to go straight from Ball to byre. Even so, getting up was like coming out of the wrong end of limbo. The black dead of night was bitter in the solid stone unheated farmhouse in a bedroom 20ft (6 metres) square and 10ft (3 metres) high even if it had a fancy Edwardian frieze round the ceiling.

'And, whativver the minister tells us, hell is COLD!'

Many farms 'took' a student for the year's practical experience required for a college degree. Learning at home, for most were farmers' sons, did not offer enough variety, nor a sufficiently impersonal assessment. Ian Grant's younger brother had gone elsewhere before the war, already determined to nail a top agri job in the Scottish Land Court since Viewfield would not be his. In time Ian's own son would be looking for a similar favour, for favour it was. There was little of direct economic value to be had from a green boy till he had been drilled into the ways of the farm. And that took time and patience.

For weeks after this particular boy started, Mrs Grant would waken in the night – she was used to it – and listen, then get up and check. Sure enough the laddie was asleep when he should have been up and out. They tried an alarm clock. He slept through that. They tried a louder one. In his sleep he reached out and turned it off. They tried two, one at the bedside and one on the chest just out of reach set for five minutes later.

Still the farmer's wife had to get up and wake him. As a last resort they added a third clock, with the loudest ring they could find, and put it inside a metal biscuit tin on the other side of the room set for five minutes later still. It was all in vain. In the end Mrs Grant removed all the clocks, taking the quietest to her own bedside. It was less bother just to get up and shake the addlehead awake. – *Margaret Woodward*

Mobile shop keeper

IT was perhaps in the 1950s that the mobile shopkeeper was at his zenith and might be reckoned along with the parson, doctor, vet, inkeeper and postmistress as a key character of the village and its surroundings. Like them, it was his job to soothe, to bring a touch of company and fun to lonely lives, to spread the gossip, and help in ways well beyond the strict course of duty.

His especial parish was those land-eating council estates built on the edge of villages in the immediate postwar years before most tenants became car owners. But from the great houses to lonely cottages, his presence was usually welcome.

The first thing that the successful mobile shopkeeper realised was that regularity seriously mattered. Without thinking, in the days when many country people told the time from the church clock (if the wind was in the right direction) or from the passage of distant trains (if it were in the other direction), everyone seemed to know exactly when the van was due. Often the dog, given a regular titbit as part of the sales pitch, was especially expectant.

The weekly itineraries had to be most carefully constructed, saving time and petrol being only one factor since catching people in was of paramount importance. That usually meant visits to larger properties, where the 'lady' would be at home, in the afternoon, while early evenings were fruitful for finding most doors answered. The mobile shopkeeper had to know when the Women's Institute and other meetings were held, when mums collected their kids from school, and much much more. Often indeed secondary weekly orders for popping through unlocked cottage doors or leaving in the garage were collected when the van 'happened' to be passing the school gates or the start of the natal clinic. An order for a heavy item collected from a woman waiting for the market day bus could give her a sense of liberation, letting her make the most of the time in town without being weighed down.

Vans were seldom new but almost always ingeniously arranged. All were instantly recognisable by their legend such as 'Bob's Mobile Shop for Value'. The goods were displayed in layers: first fresh fruit or novelty lines; then the things any housewife might be short of, prominently displayed a touch further back; finally heavy items in the rear.

The keen mobile shop owner realised that cartage was his speciality... saving housewives having to carry the really heavy items home. Prices for the heavies could afford to be a touch expensive because of the delivery service rendered. But profit naturally came from the higher priced items which might more usually be purchased on the housewife's visit to town on market day or Saturday. At least some of these had to be priced competitively.

The inside of the back doors of some vans, where the customers congregated, had their own shelves

---

Black v white

For months black American troops had been stationed in the North Devon market town of South Molton. Their place was taken with whites and the town was out of bounds to the blacks.

But one black had borrowed money from a local businessman and was honour-bound to repay it. Having furtively made his way into town, he was caught by a white soldier almost in the act of making the repayment.

The white soldier's treatment of the black enraged the townspeople whose value system put the honouring of a debt higher than any rules of out-of-bounds. Hundreds of locals crowded round the police station to which the black soldier had been taken to protest at the white troops' unfairness. The white soldiers looked on in amazement wondering why in this remote market town of all places their race should be so unpopular.

Rupert Besley

for things like flour and eggs which many might buy 'just in case' in the knowledge they would never be wasted. Chocolates and sweets were on tempting display for kids, and small bars of chocolate always accessible in a hidden compartment to give to the kids of customers specially worth cultivating.

Even if the mobile shopkeeper boasted a speciality such as greengrocer, a wide range of goods were stocked. Fish was seldom on display but in many cases might be ordered one week for delivery the next. Collecting prescriptions from town was part of the service, and some operators delivered the local newspaper quicker than the newsagent servicing the area.

What impressed one most about the displays of many vans was the prominence given to the prices. That gave an illusion of it being just like an ordinary shop where one could carefully budget. The skill on the road, however, was to get away with a penny or two extra to cover fuel and other costs, and behind the illusion of open pricing was the reality of the owner giving an instant quote for many items... dependent on the customer's means and whether the

item would sell out, become scarce or was in danger of being left as unsold stock. 'Especially for you' was a familiar phrase to tempt the purchase of an extra item that might make all the difference to the profitability of the call usually accompanied with an extra dose of gossip, perhaps a report of an elopement from the next village.

Sometimes the owners bartered, buying fresh crops from market gardeners and farmers while stretching their sales of other goods. Distributing leaflets for the vicar or social secretary was an occupational hazard.

'Save yourself the bus fare', was once a convincing argument. 'Save yourself the petrol', when families became car owners failed to make impact, for what was the point of owning a car without using it, and why not justify its use by buying more cheaply at Tescos or the International even before the days of superstores? Probably less than a tenth of the 1950s number of mobile shops survive, many of them now devoted to more specialist trades such a taking fresh fish deep into the countryside. The memory of many other drivers of mobile shops lingers on. – *David St John Thomas*

Military Records Prior to 1914

IN an article of this size it is not possible to cover every conceivable record relating to the military forces, there are just too many. This subject can also be heavy going on information, history, facts and changes so we have split it into two halves, those records prior to 1914 and the World War I, and those which we have labelled Modern Military covering 1914 up to today. This is a natural break for two reasons, the Army and Navy having undergone significant changes after this date and the Royal Air Force of course was not a separate force until 1918. Also from 1914 many personnel records and detailed information on individuals will not be available for public inspection as it will still come under the Public Record Office closure rules.

We have not differentiated between the countries which make up the United Kingdom because from 1707 the Army and Navy were administered from London. This means any Scottish ancestors you may have come across in the forces from this date forward will be found amongst those records at the Public Record Office, although there are some records at the Scottish Record Office under lists of military, naval and mercantile records. Records can be found at other repositories around the country, and these will be detailed within the article as we get to them.

History

There was no regular Standing Army across the whole country until 1660. Early defence systems were controlled on a local basis and within certain restrictions, much of it was voluntary. Prior to 1660 local armies were set up by local land owners and controlled by acts of parliament. Right from Anglo-Saxon times able-bodied men between the ages of sixteen and sixty were liable to perform some sort of military service for their local defence and occasionally when required further afield. These local forces were known as militia and records relating to them can be found in local county record offices, some larger libraries and possibly some local museums.

The Militia and Muster Rolls

The militia were in force from Anglo-Saxon times and were connected to the feudal ownership of the land. Various kings throughout history enacted royal warrants, levy systems and so on, to set down the rules by which a local defence force should exist. Up until 1660 the militia were the principal defence force of our country.

In 1660 a national standing army was set up and various voluntary companies were formed, usually from the better off members of the population, and the local militia started to fade out. These new voluntary forces however usually only existed during a threat of war or war times and were formed and disbanded as required. So once again the Militia owed its existence to an act of parliament in 1758. This put it back on a local basis and each year up until 1831 male members of the community were recruited by ballot from a list drawn up by the local constables.

Together with the Volunteers, Yeomanry and other local forces they became the home defence and until 1871 were trained

by the Lords Lieutenant of the counties. In peace time they were the responsibility of the Home Secretary but when mobilised for war, by Royal Proclamation, they came under the authority of the Commander-In-Chief.

The registers and lists of those eligible and therefore serving were called Muster Rolls/Books. Primarily they can be found locally in the county record offices, amongst the Quarter Session Records. Although there are some major sources at the PRO in London. From 1540 the records of musters were returned to the secretaries of state, and many together with some from 1522 onwards can be found.

From 1757 to 1831 they were recruited each year by ballot from parish lists of male conscripts between the ages of eighteen and fifty drawn up by the parish constables. In 1762 the upper limit was reduced to 45. The Militia ballot lists (all men) and militia enrolment lists (those men chosen to serve) should give a complete census. Any surviving lists should be found locally and can give comprehensive details on individual men and their families. During the 18th and 19th century the Militia was a county based part time force and in addition to the standing army.

Just before World War I the Militia were converted to the Special Reserve known as the Territorial Force or Territorial Army, and became a voluntary force which trained in peace time, but were drawn on at times of war. In 1942 during World War 2 another type of militia were brought back into action. They were known as the Local Defence Volunteers or Home Guard, at this time enrolment was imposed on male civilians between the ages of seventeen and 62.

Fencibles

A fencible was a soldier who was recruited purely for home service, and a group formed together were known as the local defence force. Local Volunteer fencibles were auxiliary forces under the control of the county lords lieutenant. They would train for a few weeks a year and form a local defence team in times of war. They were disbanded in 1802.

Sea fencibles were recruited in those areas around our coastline and were a type of naval militia. Between 1798 and 1810 fishermen and boatmen were recruited to form a part time coastal defence and they were usually commanded by Naval Officers. Volunteer Forces were sanctioned by the government in 1859 and were linked to the county regiments in 1872. By 1908 the volunteers and yeomanry were joined together to form a territorial force and in 1920 they were renamed the Territorial Army. Their primary task is to be a local defence force, and they train primarily at weekends. They are voluntary in as much as no one today is forced to join up, but they are paid a small allowance, and are used abroad when the need arises.

What information can you find

A lot of the records relating to the Militia and different volunteer forces can be found at the PRO in Kew, local county record offices and some

in muniment rooms attached to regimental museums.

The Militia Act laid down the minimum information that had to be provided on each man, and over the period from 1757-1832 this included names, occupations, descriptions, ages, infirmities, and the number of children over and under fourteen. They also needed to identify those men who had already served or who were eligible for exemption so extra details were added to allow them to do this. In 1806 a printed form was introduced and distributed to the households of the community. They had to fill them in and pass them back to the constable who then added them to his parish list.

Amongst the militia regimental archives you will find musters or pay lists, which only usually give a name. However, the enrolment and discharge lists can give such information as places of residence, occupations and ages.

What else should you look out for

Other records which can be found for this early military include Pension and Almsmen records of those who had retired, or were injured.

Searches can also be made of the military hospital records such as the Royal Chelsea founded in 1681 in London and the Royal Kilmainham in Dublin from 1679.

Also check the records of individual battles such as the Napoleonic Wars of 1793–1815 and Crimean 1854–1856 and Boer 1899–1902 wars. Also those records relating to prisoners of war, court martial, medals, war graves and the like.

Country Portrait

Norman Mortimore 1920–1995

NORMAN Mortimore was a known figure and good friend to both locals and newcomers alike, in the village of Throwleigh on the edge of Dartmoor. He had been a horseman and said that working with horses was more interesting than working on a tractor and not so cold, 'because you was walking behind them all the time'. Changes in farming were not all to the good as, 'They used to help one t'other, years ago. They don't help one t'other so much now: they've got the machinery and it's all for theirself'. All his life, he was interested in sheep, seeing them, as a child, on the farm of his great-uncle, Alfred Setter. Sometimes he was obliged to feel 'not very well', so that he could miss school on market – and shearing – days, as farming was always more interesting to him than school and indoor work. When he retired, he bred and showed grey-faced Dartmoor sheep, with some success, at the agricultural shows roundabout. Now, his widow, Gwen, and his son, Derek, continue to breed and show them. – *J Sarsby*

CH 2

CH 3

THE WAY WE WERE

THESE EVOCATIVE Victorian images are from our own collection of photographs taken in the 1890s. The prints are sepia duotones of the finest quality, printed on art card to ensure that the clarity and detail of the original photograph is preserved. The image size is 7ins x 5ins which is a standard frame size.

Each print is just 99p. You can order any mix, in any quantity, subject to a minimum order of 3 prints (£2.97) or order all 5 for just £4 per set, and packing and postage is FREE.

To order, write to the address below, stating the quantity and catalogue (CH) numbers you require. Cheques and postal orders should be made payable to 'The Way We

CH 4

Book Reviews

Railway Ancestors
A guide to the staff records of the railway companies of England and Wales 1822-1947
David T Hawkings
250 x 180
509 pages
Some black and white photographs and illustrations
Published by Alan Sutton Publishing Ltd
ISBN: 0-7509-0883-1
Hardback £25.00

Whether you're a railway historian/enthusiast or a family historian looking for details on members of your family who may have worked for the railway, this book is going to be a valuable guide to you. The author has already worked his way through the records and has put this guide together to help you find your way around. More than half of the book is appendicies, the first of which is a comprehensive alphabetical listing of all railway companies in England and Wales up to 1947 and nationalisation. The listing gives date of incorporation, dates of records available, details of change of ownership and the Public Record Office class where the records can be found.

In 1972 the Public Record office took over the historical records of the England and Welsh railway companies from the British Rail Records Centre, while all Scottish company records went to the Scottish Record Office in Edinburgh. The Public Record Office holds over 80,000 pieces in the form of folders, boxes and books in their RAIL section (around 2.5 miles of shelving). Records of staff are of a highly personal nature and those at the PRO which are less than 75 years old are not available for public inspection. Some staff records have also been found in some County Record Offices and this book encompasses what has been found to date and acts as a central reference source. The types of records to be found include large staff registers giving such details as full name, job title, date of birth and wages paid. Also minutes of Board meetings can be fruitful as apparently each member of staff had to be interviewed by them and in many cases each volume of minutes has been indexed. Other appendices include companies by county, railway staff records to 1923; with the GWR having its own section; staff records within the Railway Clearing House (the body who determined how much each railway Company gleaned from a through fare ticket, usually worked out by the number of miles of track); a detailed list of staff trades and occupations and a date list of major railway events. The main body of the book looks at the types of records available and through the use of illustrations and photographs gives an indication of what you might find on a search. Such records include staff registers and histories, sickness and accidents books, trade union appeals and disputes and railway magazines and newspapers. Illustrated throughout with archive documents it is an indispensable guide. At a price of £25 you may say it is a little expensive for your own library, but if you have an interest in this subject, amongst its 509 pages it has a wealth of information and assistance. Your local library should have a copy for you to look at.

Dry Stone Walls

Shire Album 114
Lawrence
Garner
210x150
32 pages
Many black
and white
photographs and
illustrations
Published by Shire Publications Ltd
ISBN 0-85263-666-0
Paperback £2.50

Dry stone walls are built with no mortar at all. Their strength and durability is purely controlled by the skill of the waller and how he places the stones locking them into place. A waller would expect his masterpiece provided they get a small amount of maintenance, to outlive him. On mountains and moorland where it is

difficult to grow vegetation and maintain other forms of fencing, a dry stone wall is a natural enclosure method with the stones of the area usually laid strewn all over the mountainside. They also provide other uses over the hedge or wire and wood fence. In lambing time they can act as shelter to the new-born lambs and ewes and of course the shepherd when up on the exposed mountains checking his flock. They also make a good firebreak and as they are usually today found in tourist areas where fires can be started carelessly, they have a practical use. They do however have their disadvantages. They are expensive to erect and compared to a wood and wire fence they take a long time to erect. A waller on his own would accomplish between 4.9 to 5.5 metres a day. This short guide with many pictures and illustrations takes you through the development and history of the dry stone wall, looking at how they are constructed, regional stones and styles used through to the craft of today. It is not a dying craft as you may think – although few new walls are being built today because of the cost of labour and stone, there are many which need repairing and restoring. In the past the trade was usually passed on from father to son, many farmers still maintaining their own walls on their land. There are organisations like the Dry Stone Walling Association which amongst other things engages in the training of wallers and has a register of professional wallers. In some parts of the country such as the Cotswolds, where there are many dry stone walls you will see the men of today putting their knowledge into practice, repairing or rebuilding existing walls. You may also see posters and advertisements in the countryside for various competitions.

Around Blandford Forum

In Old Photographs
Ben Cox
218 x 154
160 pages
Many black and white photographs
Published by Alan Sutton Publishing Ltd
ISBN 1-86299-618-X
Paperback £7.95

Blandford Forum, a market town in the Dorset countryside, was destroyed by fire in 1731 and was almost completely re-built. It became famous for its markets and sheep fairs, grammar school and breweries. It is a conservation area and has changed little from when it was re-built. Apart from three pages at the beginning which gives a brief history of Blandford, the rest of this 160 page book shows Blandford and surrounding villages in photographs through its work, military connections, sport and leisure activities and railway. Many of the photographs were taken by private individuals on glass plate or early film and it has made it difficult to date many of them. Each one has a small amount of descriptive text with an approximate date which has usually been calculated from the clothing worn or vehicles appearing in them.

The Country Garage

Shire Album 129
Llyn E Morris
210x150
32 pages
Many black and white photographs and illustrations
Published by Shire Publications Ltd
ISBN 0-85263-711-X
Paperback £2.25

The introduction of the motor car to Britain brought about a big change for rural communities, which up until then had been driven by the needs of the horse and cart, and railway. Apart from country lanes and tracks having to become solid roads or else the cars would get stuck in the mud on wet days, if the car was to be kept going it would need refuelling and maintaining. A new type of industry was moving into the countryside. The first refuelling points were at ironmongers, blacksmiths or oil shops, whilst the first maintenance shops were usually cycle shops or coach builders. Other professions also played their part and in 1899 the first 'garage' was so named. Early garages were in county or market towns to cater for those who would have a motor vehicle such as doctors and professional men. In the countryside land outside a village, alongside a busy road or cross-roads were usually the first to be erected. As farmers became more mechanised with tractors and the like country garages became more widespread, until today of course when market forces are making changes again and many country garages are in decline. This little guide takes you through the history of the country garage looking at the work carried out and by whom. If you have an interest in rural history or the history of the motor car you will find the text and many pictures a mine of information.

Criminal Ancestors
A guide to historical criminal records in England and Wales
David T Hawkings
244 x 171
462 pages

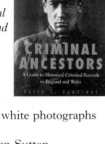

Some black and white photographs and illustrations
Published by Alan Sutton Publishing Ltd
ISBN: 0-7509-1084-4
Paperback £14.99

The thought to many of us of having at least one criminal ancestor is disbelief. But it is likely that many of us have, not because they were naughty or evil, but in many instances, just so that they could survive. Using information held by county/borough records offices, the Public Record Office, police archives, and a case study this book shows to what extent one individual criminal can be researched. The author himself found at least one ancestor to have been imprisoned for fourteen days in 1851 for stealing fifteen pieces of firewood, but further research into jail records also gave a description of the person, how old he was and the fact he was married and where he lived at the time. All useful information to a family historian. It concentrates on the legal system of England and Wales for the 16th to 19th centuries and provides a guide for those wishing to use the criminal records for research purposes. The statements of defendants, victims and witnesses contain all sorts of details to the researcher revealing what life must have been like then. Numerous examples of different types of records are used throughout showing the way they were written and presented. It covers prisons, criminal courts, transportation, Home Office documents recording criminals, the Director of Public Prosecutions, bankrupts and debtors. The appendices cover what is held at the Public Record Office and other repositories which give details of individuals.

Rough Justice

The celebrated 'hanging judge', Lord Braxfield, is reputed to have said to a prisoner to the bar, who had been pleading his own case with remarkable eloquence and astuteness – 'Ye're a very clever chiel; but ye wad be nane the waur o' a hanging.' – *RM*

Books of the past

WHETHER you are a hunting, shooting and fishing person or not, if you have a deep and abiding passion for the countryside you will know that the initials 'BB' stand for far more than a comfortable bed and full English breakfast at some friendly hostelry. The initials are the pseudonym of the great countryside writer Denys Watkins-Pitchford who not only wrote with the very essence of the countryside flowing from his pen but also illustrated his books, using his real name as artist, to perfection.

When reading a 'BB' book it is easy to become side-tracked by the

Pheasant on Exmoor: *Trevor Beer*

excellent illustrations, to explore the hedgerows, fields and lanes searching for the pheasants, rabbits and other creatures to be found. Wonderful work and truly atmospheric.

Denys Watkins-Pitchford was born in 1905, growing up in a Northamptonshire village where he spent many hours in the open air fighting illness as a boy. He then went on to study art in Paris and at The Royal College of Art in London. For seventeen years he was art master at Rugby school, first using the famous 'BB' initials in 1937 for *The Sportsman's Bedside Book*. This was followed by *Wild Lone, The Story of a Pytchley Fox* (1939) and *Manka The Sky Gypsy, The Story of a Wild Goose* (1939). Then in 1941 came *The Little Grey Men* the tale of the last gnomes in England for which he was awarded the Carnegie Medal.

Many contributions to *The Field, Country Life* and *Shooting Times* built his reputation as a field naturalist and 'BB' who died in 1990, will be read far and wide during the 21st century without doubt.

Other books by 'BB' include *The Fisherman's Bedside Book* and *The Birdlover's Bedside Book*. Search the bookshops or look for reprints now becoming available for this fine country author's work. – *Trevor Beer*

REFLECTIONS

The Way We Used to Live

'Spasms'

FARMER HEMMANT paused in mid flow, his shiny pint ladle half way between his two gallon galvanised milk churn and mother's blue and white banded quart pitcher. To her astonishment he hooked the ladle back into the pail, closed the half flap and set down her jug on the doorstep.

She asked him what was the matter. He smiled, put his finger to his lips and in the silence the Westminster chiming clock struck twelve. When it finished, he sighed and asked if he could see it. At this point, young Billy moved out of sight for Farmer Hemmant had often chased him out of mushroom fields and had put in a bull to stop future depradations.

Ernest John Reed (1930-31) (Note the solid tyred lorry)

Ernest John Reed, the author's father, 1943

He gazed lovingly at the handsome wooden cased clock, nearly 18ins long. Although it added a certain dignity, it was out of place on the small mantelpiece of the council house living room. Mother told him Father had won it in a magazine competition. She did not know if her husband would sell it, but she would be glad to be rid of it. The chimes worried her and it was too big for the mantelpiece.

So the farmer took Dad over the back meadow to Castle Farm, so named because of the brick built castellated tower constructed on the site of an ancient fortification. There he showed him his collection of about fifty clocks, and eventually bought the Westminster chimes for five pounds, a sum which would take two weeks to earn. As the only bread-winner with a growing and always hungry family to feed and clothe Dad was glad to turn the timepiece into money.

The competitions appeared in *Pearsons Weekly* and *Tit Bits* as well as *John Bull* and other papers. While *John Bull* called its competition *Bullets*, others used *Nuggets*, *Trebles*, or *Trumps*. Entrants were given phrases to which they added short rejoinders. Father won ten pounds for TOO ABSURD – Airman expecting 'Walkover', five guineas for OUTSTANDING – 'Land-marks' in Naval History and five pounds for SO CONVINCING – Marksman without 'Buts'. His other prizes included many cash amounts ranging from 2/6d to £10, a portable gramophone, a 'desk reference atlas', several Christmas turkeys, a Christmas hamper, a 'wristlet watch', a 3/- book of stamps, and tinned chicken and ham. The letter which accompanied the meats issued patro-nising instructions as to their use.

Compared with many competi-tions today, these older ones required intelligence and wit, although luck must have played its part in the shape of the preferences of the judges. Prizes were good, for the maximum was usually £250, still a large sum in the fifties when the magazines began to fold. There were many smaller awards. One list shows four large sum prizes, five 'Spring outfits', fifty small cash prizes and a hundred sixpenny vouchers for the next entry fee. The clientele was from all over England, Scotland and Wales, including Clergy and about 20 percent of female winners.

Dad called the exercise his 'spasms' and kept paper and pencil in his pocket, or beside the bed so that inspiration could be captured before it departed for limbo. Mother knew that odd scraps of scribbled paper must never be destroyed. They might turn into cash. Evenings were often spent transcribing worthwhile ideas into a small pocket book. There was no money for the entertainments of the nearby town so we enjoyed the winter nights with Ludo and other board games, conversation, the wireless and 'spasms'. - *Frank Reed*

The Phantom Pig

'SHIRLEY!' Come away from the window.' The commanding voice of her mother went unheeded by the little girl kneeling on a chair, craning her neck to see the corner of the farmyard where a large pink, muddied pig was being dragged and pushed by several men towards a small shed.

The area in front of the dark wooden building was concreted, sloping to a central drain, and something of unusual interest must be about to take place; and, adding to her determination to stay deaf, one which the grown-ups did not wish her to see or they would all have been in the yard to watch.

Her grandmother's firm hands took her around the waist and she was lifted down, facing the small brick-floored cottage kitchen, with its black range and sparse furnishing. A large mesh guard prevented her and her toddling brother from getting too close to the fire, and she was encouraged to join him at play on the rag hearthrug where her plaster-headed doll, with its moulded hair, lay in a jumble of coloured wooden bricks and cloth books.

Loud squealing from the struggling pig, competed with whistling tones from the turned-up wireless, from where 'Here comes the army Mr Brown' suddenly sung out clearly as the yard went silent. Shirley rushed to the window. A quick glance before being dragged away revealed a pool of red on the concrete and glimpses of the pig, now feet up, through the hurrying legs of the men as they dragged the carcass out of sight.

The pump handle worked hard that afternoon. Buckets clanged and water swished. When they finally went for a late walk a strong smell of singeing roused distant memories, as, turning her brother's pushchair quickly away from the direction of the shed, her mother hurried them away. All her interested questions unanswered, Shirley could only await with suppressed excitement the arrival of darkness, the lumpy, ill-wrapped package hastily handed to her mother and pork for lunch on Sunday.

Reminded at bedtime never to talk of the pig or the afternoon's events, she would have been puzzled to see, late that night, the familiar shape of

'Old George' silhouetted against the light streaming from the farmhouse back door. With a bulky parcel under his arm, he wheeled his well oiled bike into the lane, and mounted shakily, the darkness quickly absorbing all but the polished badge on his tall dark helmet. – *Nancy Nicholl*

The Farm Dog

ONLY Old Bob was allowed indoors. The other farm dogs would've had a besom up their backsides had they tried it. But then, Shep and Bess, the collies, and Teak, the feisty Jack Russell, who nipped fear-

Bob, the farm dog

lessly in and out of bovine hooves and hurled himself recklessly at the biggest of rats, would have scorned such luxury.

Old Bob could steer the flock efficiently enough (provided no 'yo' turned and stamped her foot at him), but he was no guard dog. Devout coward and incurable hypochondriac, he liked his creature comforts and knew only too well the power of a forlorn whimper, a half-raised paw and a pitiful look.

Perhaps it was because we children had nursed him so tenderly through illness and accident – real and imaginary - that the farmer and his wife turned a blind eye when Bob slithered in, bent-legged and grinning, and made for his bit of sack by the range.

Besides, he was always good for a laugh. His favourite trick was putting things in silly places: a lump of coal in an untended basket, a bit of old bone in a bucket or churn and once, a rubber ball in the scuttle. Too bad the embers were still hot and the ball evaporated into a spiral of acrid smoke.

Unlike the other dogs, who considered such things beneath them, Old Bob was always ready for a game. First there was Pooh Sticks, which he invented all by himself.

The Long Meadow dropped steeply down to a small stream and, after rain, water cascaded down the furrows like miniature rapids.

Old Bob would drop a stick into the gushing water, race it all the way down to the bottom, then, with a triumphant yap, snatch it up and hurtle back up the hill for another go.

But it was another game altogether that saved our Doreen.

One of our favourite haunts was Tally Woods where, in a single afternoon, we'd hunt deer with King Henry, deliver fair maidens from Black Knights and massacre whole tribes of Indians.

As we whooped and charged through the woods, our Doreen, younger than us and a girl to boot, puffed and whimpered behind us, struggling to keep up. Until one day she didn't.

It wasn't 'til teatime that we discovered she was missing. We weren't supposed to take our Doreen into the woods - there were badger sets for her to tumble down, rabbit holes to catch unwary legs and boulders to bark tender shins. Taking her with us would earn us a clip round the ear: coming home without her didn't bear contemplating.

It was Bernard who thought of it. Slipping into the farmhouse, he stole one of our Doreen's socks from the wash basket, whistled for Old Bob and back we raced to the woods.

Bernard wrapped the sock round Old Bob's muzzle. 'Find it, Bob! Find it!' Old Bob looked puzzled for a moment and our hearts sank, but then light seemed to dawn and off he raced...

We threatened her with all sorts not to split, but her tear- streaked face told its own story and that night we felt the back of the farmer's hand.

Old Bob, curled as usual on his bit of sack, felt it, too, but gently, behind one ear. Strangely, this, to us, seemed a fair exchange.

Happiest Days...

THEY were, so they said, the happiest days of your life. Schooldays: eight or nine years (if you were lucky) before you were despatched into service or apprenticeship and, at fourteen, childhood ended, officially and abruptly.

Tuition may have been free, but little else was. You could, for 2d a week, have a bowl of hot soup at lunchtime; most chose to bring sandwiches and a spoonful of sugar and cocoa powder done up in a twist of brown paper and queue for a mug of hot water to mix it in.

Milk, a third of a pint in miniature bottles, was a ha'penny a day, but the dexterous certainly got their money's worth: the cardboard tops were speared and used as a base for woollen pom-poms for your hair or the new baby's bonnet. Or you could join them together and wrap round and round with raffia to make a table mat for Mum.

Uniforms were - well, uniform. No designer jeans or fancy trainers then. Instead, serge gym slips for the girls, hateful woollen stockings and flannelette bloomers with a pocket for your clean hanky. For boys, short trousers made for marbled knees in winter and for both, long combinations with three buttons across the backside for strategic undoing. Thick and scratchy, they were known universally as 'itchy coos' and as universally loathed.

Discipline was strict. Caning was commonplace and woe betide you if Pa found out or you'd get another wallop when you got home, 'to go with it'.

But there was still a playground, where girls played hopscotch, grandmother's footsteps, Jacks and skipping, all in deadly, squabbly earnest.

Boys had marbles, footballs made from tightly rolled up newspaper and, in due season, conkers, the cause of many a split finger and not a few black eyes.

The 4 o'clock bell signalled hometime and a walk, for some, of several miles. If Mum had banked up the fire in readiness, it might be toast for tea, singed and tasting of coal dust, with a smear of dripping and thick, yellow milk straight from the cow.

Later, if you were lucky, you could huddle up to the wireless and thrill to the latest adventures of *Dick Barton Special Agent*.

But Saturday nights were favourites. After a good scrub in preparation for Sunday Chapel, clatter downstairs in pyjamas and slippers, and huddle round the fire, jockeying for position nearest the wireless. Anxious moments while Pa fiddled unnecessarily with the knob, then the moment we'd all been waiting for: those opening bars of 'Violets, sweet violets' and the beginning of 'In Town Tonight'. After that, (so long as Max Miller wasn't on – he was considered too vulgar for tender ears), there was 'Music Hall' with Gert and Daisy, Gracie Fields and the Two Leslies.

They were the days, so they said, of innocence and industry. And, perhaps, after all, they were right. – *Valerie Jones*

The Norfolk Giant

ROBERT Hales of West Somerton in Norfolk was know as 'The Norfolk Giant' because he stood 7ft 8in and weighed more than 32st. By the age of four he looked like a ten-year old, and at nine he stood almost 6ft.

The son of a farmer, Robert was born in 1820 and according to the records he was 'of the most courteous and gentle disposition, most genial and generous', which endeared him to everyone.

With his diminutive sister Mary (she was 7ft 2in), Robert toured Britain and America appearing at country fairs and shows, and met Queen Victoria who declared herself to be 'most charmed by the tall gentleman'.

Robert died on November 22 1863 and his enormous tomb, topped by a sarcophagus-like memorial, now attracts tourists to the peaceful churchyard of rural St Mary at West Somerton. – *Carl Hughes*

The tomb of Norfolk giant Robert Hales at West Somerton, Norfolk

Fascinating Follies

Jeffrey W Whitelaw

A Folly has been defined as a useless building erected for ornament on a gentleman's estate and, indeed, some of the finest follies are to be found in the great landscaped gardens of Stowe, Stourhead, Shugborough and so on - the final outcome when rich landowners, after returning from making the Grand Tour of Europe in the 18th century, decided to improve the look of their estates by the addition of sham ruins, temples and other eye-catchers.

Many follies, however, exist outside the great gardens and can sometimes be found standing in isolation - with no apparent reason for why they are in that particular spot - and, although some were probably built to give employment in hard times, many just satisfied a whim of their creator or commemorated a great event.

The Sham Ruin, Mount Edgcumbe, Cornwall:
The Park and the gardens at Mount Edgcumbe, the earliest landscaped park in Cornwall, have been owned jointly by Cornwall County Council and Plymouth City Council since 1971: the public are free to walk its entirety and see, among other structures, this sham ruin of circa 1750 overlooking Plymouth Sound. This folly, originally an eye-catcher for Mount Edgcumbe House, was thought to have been built with stones and window fitments from a demolished church, but there is no proof of this. In the Park there is also Milton's Temple, an Orangery and an elaborate Italian-style garden with statues.

Panorama Tower, Croome Park, Worcestershire:
Croome Court is the former home of the Earls and Countesses of Coventry, where Lancelot 'Capability' Brown was employed to design the Park - it is considered to be his most influential creation - and Robert Adam to garnish it with 'picturesque buildings'. Croome Park has now been bought by the National Trust, and in time The Orangery (known as The Temple Greenhouse), a grotto, The Rotunda (a garden pavilion) and other follies will be open to view. However, the Panorama Tower, an eyecatcher, now stands in a field away from the Park - separated from it, in fact, by the building of the M5 Motorway.

Rousham Eyecatcher, Steeple Aston, Oxfordshire:
William Kent designed the gardens at Rousham House in 1737 and, unlike so many other designs of the 18th century, they remain today almost as planned. To complete his scheme, he built this eyecatcher - more a screen than a sham castle but one of the earliest of the sham ruins - to be seen from the house although it was outside the immediate perimeter. It is visible from the road from Hopcrofts to Lower Heyford, but a closer view is possible from a track leading out of the village of Steeple Aston.

Dunstall Castle, Defford, Worcestershire: This massive sham castle stands right beside the road on Dunstall Common, at Defford south-west of Pershore. This folly was, for many years, considered to be part of the follies erected for Croome Park but, although within sight of the Park, it is not now thought to be one of Robert Adam's creations and so its purpose and its builder remain a mystery.

The Triangular Lodge, Rushton, Northamptonshire: The Lodge was built between 1593 and 1595 in the grounds of Rushton Hall, near Kettering, by Sir Thomas Tresham. Sir Thomas, although brought up as a Protestant, became a Catholic and was imprisoned for his beliefs: whilst in prison he became obsessed with the Holy Trinity and this obsession caused him to erect the Triangular Lodge where everything is in odd numbers, mainly threes, trefoils and divisions of three.

The Gothic Temple, Stowe, Buckinghamshire: The gardens at Stowe, in which can be seen work by Charles Bridgeman, James Gibbs, William Kent and 'Capability' Brown, were acquired by the National Trust in 1989. They contain 37 Grade 1 listed temples, monuments, a Palladian Bridge and many smaller follies. The Gothic Temple, designed by Gibbs circa 1740-1745, is arguably the best building in the gardens: it has now been restored and rooms have been constructed inside so that the Landmark Trust can let it as a holiday home.

AMBASSADORS FOR YORKSHIRE LIFE AND TRADITION

Marie Hartley and Joan Ingilby

FOR fifty years, Marie Hartley and Joan Ingilby have been writing books together – and in Marie Hartley's case, also photographing and illustrating – about the people of Yorkshire, their social history and their ways of life. Their partnership began with *The Old-Hand-Knitters of the Dales*, which was published in 1951, and they went on to produce books every two or three years, (as well as numerous articles in magazines,) until, by 1997, they had published over twenty titles together, and were still writing. Their work has always had a tremendous following: they have a zest for their subject, a respect, but also a lightness of touch, with humour and sharpness of observation, and a keen interest in people, as well as in the discoverable facts and artifacts of history. Writing of their work on the hand-knitters of the Dales, they admitted to a greater interest in the knitters themselves than the craft. One can detect their delight when they heard the knitter, Mrs Crabtree, say,...'My Mother's needles fair made music'..., when describing her mother's knitting skills.

Their next book, *Yorkshire Village* (1953), was a history of Askrigg, the village in Wensleydale, which they had made their home, and although it was a village study, their approach was anything but narrow or parochial. They scoured the Diocesan records, braved the dust and damp of sacks of aged documents in the Church Institute at Leeds (later feeling off-colour), visited the British Library, the Public Record Office and Trinity College, Cambridge – following the trail of history wherever it led, but also realising that clues to the past could be found, not just in documents, but '...in the meadows and pasture, lanes and buildings, wherever there are the traces of man...', and also in the memories of people.

They followed this study with a broader canvas, a guide book, *The Yorkshire Dales* (1956), which was described by *Country Life* as '...a model of what a guide book should be', and, later, by the *Belfast Newsletter* as 'Truly a marvellous seven-shillings worth'. In 1995, in *Fifty Years in the Yorkshire Dales*, Marie Hartley and Joan Ingilby described how they worked, walking and exploring, meeting people and listening to their stories. They talked to Miss Calvert, who described how she walked, as an eight-year old in the 1870s, from Burnley to Gunnerside to the Methodist Midsummer Festival, '...how she had run about picking up goose feathers, and had sat on the pastures which were 'clad with people'...Betsy Parrington of Dent told them about the popularity of Dent Fair '...when stalls lined the streets and you could walk on people's heads'...In the snippets of remembered conversations, one catches their excitement, reaching back into the living past through encounters with people's memories. *The Wonders of Yorkshire* (1959), *Yorkshire Portraits* (1961) and *Getting to Know Yorkshire* (1964), a book for children, followed.

One of their most fascinating books – illustrated with Marie Hartley's remarkable photographs and clear, careful drawings – is *Life and Tradition in the Yorkshire Dales*, (1968), republished by Smith Settle in 1997. The way of life in the Dales had changed and most of the rural skills were dying; they described themselves as being 'just in the nick of time' to be able to find people with these fast-disappearing skills. They found farms where there were still working horses. They found farmers who still cut peat for the fire, a few women who were cheese or butter-makers, some blacksmiths and shoe-makers, cloggers and saddlers, many joiners and masons who had skills in wood and stone, and people who could revive skills with old, discarded tools -the 'backcan'

Marie Hartley (right) and Joan Ingilby at the Ryedale Folk Museum, Hutton-le-Hole, while researching for *Life and Tradition in the Moorlands of North-East Yorkshire, 1971* - T Geoffrey Willey

tinsmith and the wheelwright, whose work had been laid aside.

In order to make drawings of these crafts, they became collectors of bygones from farmhouse, barn and dairy, scanning the adverts in the local papers for sales all over the Dales. They would spend hours waiting for a particularly desired item to come up, or negotiating with buyers, who wanted only the modern objects in a sale lot and would part with the old things for a few shillings.

They visited folk-museums, photographed in farm-kitchens and dairies, and found subjects for their photographs on their walks and expeditions: a farmer mending a

In October 1967 Marie Hartley and Joan Ingilby spent three days watching William Thomas Thompson in his workshop at Hawes Town Head making a cart wheel for a Dales cart. This picture shows a wheel in place on a wheel stool. Setting out for size with callipers for the diameter of the naf (hub), which is ten inches. Mark off the naf centre. From *Making a Cartwheel*

wall, and a group of men, clipping sheep on the summit of Buttertubs Pass. Two brothers, John and Richard Wallbank showed them how they used to salve a sheep, and their cousin, William Wallbank of Keasden near Settle, described the huge gatherings of men, who used to come together to clip the sheep – at a time, he said, when work and pleasure were not separate – as they are, all too often, in farming today.

An interesting aside to this delightful study of local rural life, caught in decline and in transition to a more uniform modernity, is the mention (in *Fifty Years in the Yorkshire Dales*) that they went to visit Hannah Hauxwell at Low Birk Hatt, the 'old-fashioned lady', who was to become so famous on television, eight years later, but who declined, at that time, to be photographed. She offered to loan them an old type of butter-churn, a stand churn, which they had wanted to buy, and it is intriguing to learn that it is now on loan to the Dales Countryside Museum at Hawes, for which the authors' collection of farm, kitchen and dairy equipment formed the basis of the museum's collection. Two rooms and a small barn had housed their 'bygones', mostly amassed while they were researching *Life and Tradition in the Yorkshire Dales*, and in 1972, they felt that 'something had to be done about them' – a decision which led to their offering them to the then North Riding County Council for a public museum. The problem of the lack of a suitable site was eventually solved when the Yorkshire Dales National Park, which had bought the station at Hawes, offered the goods warehouses to house the museum. Money was found and grant aid followed.

Life and Tradition in the Yorkshire Dales was the first of three 'traditions' books, and was followed by *Life and Tradition in the Moorlands of North-East Yorkshire* (1972) and *Life and Tradition in West Yorkshire* (1976), which, together, show the amazing diversity of rural and industrial Yorkshire, and the vitality of West Yorkshire before the 1980s. All are now reprinted by Smith Settle of Otley in West Yorkshire.

This year, Marie Hartley and Joan Ingilby have produced, with their

In 1966 Marie Hartley and Joan Ingilby photographed Jim Peacock (1908–1981), stonemason at Castle Bolton in Wensleydale, working at the banker (work bench) near his home.

This picture shows the mason's tools: steel set square, chisels including pitch tool, punch, boaster, mallet made of beechwood, and hammer for use on the punch. From *Making Stonework*

publisher, six little books in a series called *Making A...* which are based on the photographs of craftworkers which Marie Hartley took in the 1960s. They follow, photographically, the processes of making – a backcan, cheese and butter, a cartwheel, boots, shoes and clogs – step by step, as they saw them in workshops, thirty years ago. Each book focuses on one type of craft or skill, and is most successful when it deals with just one process – the volume on stonework is perhaps a little too broad a subject to cover in a pocketbook of this kind, while the process of making a backcan (in *Making a*

Backcan) is vividly portrayed, and the women cheese and butter-makers in their flowered dresses and pinnies are a delight. These books would be ideal accompaniments to a visit to the

Boot-maker Tommy Hunter of Red-mire, aged 86, as one of a series of boot and shoemakers interviewed and photographed by the authors in the mid sixties. Here, nails are being put into a boot sole. Note the rack for lasts, and below a bench for customers and friends. From *Making a Boots, Shoes & Clogs*

displays of the skills and artifacts of rural life at the museum at Hawes.

In 1994, their publishers, Smith Settle, brought out *A Favoured Land, Yorkshire in Text and Image*, which was a survey and appreciation of the work of Marie Hartley and Joan Ingilby, their joint writing and Marie Hartley's illustrations. It was equally an appreciation of her first partnership with Ella Pontefract, who wrote six books accompanied by Marie Hartley's wood engravings and drawings, before her early death

in 1945. After her death, Marie Hartley wrote *Yorkshire Heritage* (1950) as a tribute to her, and from then on, realising she could write as well as illustrate, became a co-author as well as illustrator. Joan Ingilby had joined her in 1947, and *Fifty Years in the Yorkshire Dales* (1995), describes their lives and their work together over the last fifty years. *A Favoured Land* allows one a glimpse of each of their books, their subject matter and illustrations, reminding one, at the same time, of the attention which Marie Hartley's engravings,

In 1965 the authors spent a day with Frank Shields, who lived at Redmire, and had his workshop in the upper story of a barn near Bolton Castle. Although he had not practised his craft of tinsman since World War 2, he made them a backcan.

Here, he is putting the tin through rollers twice to 'break' the tin and leave it in a curve. The bright sides are then out together, which become the outside. From *Making a Backcan*

lino-cuts, drawings, photographs and paintings have attracted in recent years. The tributes of Hilary

In the 1960s, when cheese and butter-making had almost faded away, the authors photographed a number of Dales women making cheese and butter. Here, Mrs W Mason of Lodge Hall, Ribblesdale, churns cream in an end-over-end churn. From *Making Cheese and Butter*

Diaper, Mary Farnell, Gordon Forster and Joan Thirsk also remind the reader of the respect and affection in which their work is held among historians of social history, both urban and agricultural, and among art historians and photographers, who share the same enthusiasm to understand and record disappearing communities, skills and ways of life, so that they are not entirely lost to new generations.- *Jacqueline Sarsby*

Countryside and Community Research Unit, CGCHE

The series, *Making A...*is published by Smith Settle, Ilkley Road, Otley, West Yorkshire LS21 3JP. tel. 01943 467 958 or fax 10943 850057.

There are six titles so far: *Backcan, Cartwheel, Stonework, Ironwork, Boots and Shoes, Cheese and Butter*, all 158 x 158mm, 48 pages with 40 b&w photographs, paperback and costing £2.95 each.

At Hawes in 1996, RB Spencer, aged 89, still worked at the smithy. When he was fifteen, he was apprenticed to John Oswald Dinsdale, working from 8am until 7pm, and starting at 8/- a week. The smith stands by while customer Frank Outhwaite tests the angle of the scythe blade to the handle. Notice the grass nail joining the handle and blade. From *Making Ironwork*

Special Christmas Offer

Treat yourself or solve a Christmas gift problem by buying a complete set of all nine of our previous issues, with index, for just £19.95, including p&p. Single issues can be individually bought at £3.25 inc p&p. **The index to issues numbered 1-9 will be available shortly priced £2.50 if purchased separately**.

Issue 1

Issue 2

Issue 3

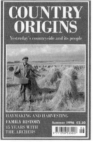

Issue 4

Issue 5

Issue 6

Issue 7

Issue 8

Issue 9

Send to: Back Issues, COUNTRY ORIGINS, PO Box 4, Nairn IV12 4HU

REFLECTIONS

The Way We Used to Travel

God's Wonderful Railway

OF all the special issues of *The Times* that have survived in quantity in personal collections, that celebrating the Great Western Railway's centenary in 1935 is probably the most popular. The writer has personally been shown carefully-preserved copies among the papers of literally dozens of people alive and dead, most of them not real railway enthusiasts but respectful of the unique history and character of God's Wonderful Railway.

Twenty eight broadsheet pages are crammed with details of the GWR's uniqueness... its original broad gauge, its speed, its pioneering in many respects, its complex integration of main lines and branches, stations great and small, hotels (including that at Paddington which when built was the largest in the Empire) and its docks (the largest dock system under single ownership in Europe).

The headings tell the tale. 'Brunel's Abiding Monument', 'Foresight and Adventure', 'Romance of Swindon', 'Historic Journeys', 'Landscape and Architecture', plus a series dealing with social, housing and recreation aspects of the company's activities.

The only railway to preserve its identity in the 1923 grouping, the Great Western set out to be a legend in its own time, public relations usually coming directly under the Superintendent of the Line. The publicity machine was amazing. There were books for Boys of All Ages, the first-ever displayed newspaper advertisement, jig-saw puzzles that are still collectors' pieces and, in the restaurant car, Great Western whisky and Great Western assorted biscuits.

Several key points emerge. First, the management so enjoyed the confidence of its staff that when any change was announced there was a general expectation it would be an improvement... so different from

Opposite above **The essence of Great Western. 1025am at Paddington and so a few minutes before the departure of the Cornish Riviera Express making the world's longest non-stop train journey in 1934 as it did with similar appearance well after postwar nationalisation.**

Opposite below **A reminder that the Great Western was the Royal Road, King George VIs funeral train leaving Paddington. Queen Victoria took her first train journey to Paddington.**

later days. Secondly the railway was seen as romantic, and interest in it as good for business. The policy was ever open. There was great continuity: engines of the same basic shape pulled main line trains from the end of the last century until the finish of steam in the 1960s. Yet the railway led the world in many respects, including the Automatic Train Control system which helped achieve a safety record unbeaten in the entire history of transport systems.

If you had to choose just one of the GWR's claims to fame, it would have to be its esprit de corps. It was

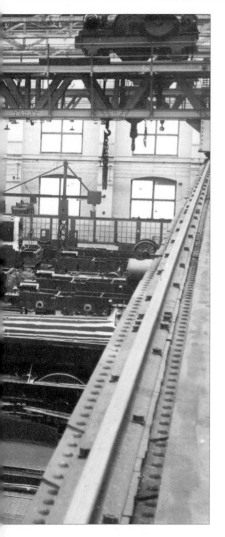

A group of those famous tapering boilers of Great Western locomotives within Swindon works. If you worked here, you were 'inside', as opposed to the 'outside' of the rest of mortals. The children of insiders were expected to do better at school.

Right until nationalisation in 1948, the first train from Cornwall did not reach Paddington until the last one of the day was on its way back, making day trips impossible. Against which, many of today's trains still take longer en route than sixty years ago.

One other measure of the Great Western's success is the extent to which parts are still preserved. Indeed, no other commercial enterprise in the history of man has proved anything like as collectable - or been so written about. Preservation includes several whole branch lines, now major tourist attractions, as well as Kings, Castles and other locomotive classes, while *The Times* centenary supplement is just one of hundreds of publications (evacuation timetables are another) still in wide circulation. – *David St John Thomas*

The junction refreshment room

At junctions between secondary and even more minor branches there were long gaps without activity. The station cat slept in the sun while staff busied themselves in a score of ways having nothing to do with railway employment. The signalman might restore bicycles at the foot of the steps leading down from his box as a profitable sideline, the stationmaster perhaps even went fishing, the porter

revered as much by its staff as by the public to whom it pandered.

Was it all justified? Was it really so great a railway? Compared with others, yes, but in truth real expresses were thin on the tracks and the average speed and comfort of other services was not in the same league.

rabbit hunting. Then, suddenly, trains would approach from several directions at once. Everything came madly to life, the cat scarpered, the signalman ran up and down the steps between pulling levers and exchanging bell codes and collecting and handing the single-line tokens to engine drivers, tickets were collected, luggage exchanged between trains and pushed into the parcels office... until the trains had gone on their way, the signals returned to stop, and even the cat went back to sleep.

The refreshment rooms at such stations were an especially colourful concern, part of the countryside itself and yet strangely remote from it in some ways... especially at stations which could only be reached and left by train or a long walk across the fields as there was no road access. Dovey Junction, where the lines to Aberystwyth and north further along the Cambrian coast, was one such station, situated on a marsh subject to flooding and commanding a fine view of bird and other wildlife.

Especially in winter, the gaps between trains were huge, but when several arrived in quick succession, and in summer these could include really long ones, queues quickly formed at the counters as passengers doused their thirst and attempted to satisfy their hunger.

At such stations many passengers were refreshed during the brief change of trains, while others darted in hoping for quick service while a loved one hopefully kept a carriage door open to prevent their being left behind. In those days country trains were slower, there were rarely refreshments on board (and the perhaps once-daily restaurant car served only full meals out of the range of most country folk), so grabbing a drink was especially important. Those in the know positioned themselves so their carriage would stop opposite the refreshment room.

At a few stations, special refreshment stops were made. Crianlarich, roughly half way between Glasgow and Fort William, was one where trains were usually allocated ten minutes and everyone poured into the diminutive eating establishment at once. To be in charge of such a refreshment room meant being equally able to handle the pressure several times a day and cope with the boredom of the rest – once the washing up had been done.

Back to the Cambrian lines, another remarkable refreshment room was at Moat Lane Junction, where the Mid-Wales line took off for its southerly treck toward Brecon. Here it was the usual pattern of rushes between long lulls, but late running of connecting trains in the war plus of course military traffic produced much extra business and strain. The story has already been told of how the manager handed a telegram from a soldier to his dear one to see if anyone else could decipher the words of love.

Dovey and Moat Lane Junctions have long been closed, while Crianlarich is a good example of a refreshment room that has survived under a series of private managements and now enjoys the support of many passing motorists. – *David St John Thomas*

The Bicycle

A B Demaus

AT the time when Queen Victoria's long reign began, land transport was dominated by the horse, but it ended with the supremacy of the iron horse, for the 20th century dawned with a countrywide network of railways and a railway service that was the envy of the world. However, it was the efficiency of the railways that served to relegate the roads to a state of shameful neglect. The dominance of the horse entailed a whole social system devoted to the continuation of that dominance. It was a sizeable section of society that devoted any threat to its own interests.

It was the bicycle that first posed that threat. Although the bicycle in its earliest 'boneshaker' forms was seen at first as little more than a fad that would be unlikely to last, the development of the graceful 'Ordinary Bicycle', which came to be disparagingly known as 'Penny-Farthing', and the many forms of tricycle that were available by the 1880s, proved that the 'fad' had a following that was growing very rapidly.

Less tangibly, attitudes were changing too. The spread of railways made travel easier and much quicker, and, to many, more desirable. But the railways still tied the traveller to set routes and times. By contrast, the bicycle or tricycle allowed complete freedom of choice as to times, routes and destinations, a freedom that increasingly seemed to be a desirable factor in life. But there were still social restrictions that had to be overcome.

The high 'Ordinaries', with their front wheels anything up to sixty or more inches in diameter and their saddles at approximately shoulder

Overleaf **This is a particularly evocative picture of motoring in the pioneer days. Mr & Mrs Pritchard of Hereford are out driving their 1904 1.6-litre single-cylinder Oldsmobile 'Curved Dash' model, registered CJ 445 in Hereford, on a fine day in early summer. The site is Green Crize, a few miles outside the City of Hereford. The 'Curved Dash' Oldsmobile was the world's first mass-production car. Note the absence of weather protection for driver and passenger, other than a rug wrapped round their knees, and gloves. The car was bought second-hand for £15.**

Mr Pritchard was a pioneer cyclist, motor-cyclist and motorist, and also an early aviator.

The stone-knapper about his task in the foreground is a reminder both of how road surfacing material was obtained in the early days and of the state of rural roads at the time.

Mr R Dresser, of Bognor, Sussex, got his wife to photograph him on tricycle... on solid tyres, of course, in the country in the summer of 1883

height to a standing man, were strictly for males only. Tricycles were heavy machines and although ladies did ride them, only the most enthusiastic ladies went far afield. The magic key that was to open the flood-gates to the freedom of the road had yet to appear.

The tall and speedy 'Ordinary' appealed little to the timid or non-athletic rider and by the mid-1880s designs of small-wheeled, 'dwarf' machines began to appear. These were termed 'safeties', a reflection of the fact that many a rider had come a cropper over the handlebars of the flying high-wheelers. Safety designs multiplied, some of them with odd and complex springing features designed to reduce the jolts to the rider caused by appalling road surfaces and solid tyres.

John Dunlop had, in 1888, made practical the invention of the pneumatic tyre. Within a very few years its advantages, despite the then common drawback of punctures, had become so obvious that earlier forms of tyre rapidly faded from the scene. The pneumatic tyre, to quote a contemporary source, 'added wings to one's wheels'. It did more than anything else to make the freedom of individual road travel not only desirable but feasible for all. Now the ladies could escape the good intentions of their chaperones and share their cycling leisure with their male counterparts.

The growth in the pastime of cycling drew attention to many deficiencies that the new mode of travel laid open. Cyclists began to see the need to take co-ordinated action to try to improve their lot. Foremost among the bids to achieve this end was the foundation of the Bicycle Touring Club on 5 August 1878.

Support for this organisation had grown enough to warrant a change of name to Cyclists' Touring Club in 1883, by which time its membership had grown to 10,627. It was not influential enough to campaign vigorously

A typical male cyclist and his 'Ordinary' of about 1885. Such machines were only suitable for male riders. Note that the saddle is at shoulder height and the only brake is a primitive 'spoon' acting on the front (solid) tyre.

Above Mrs Townsend, of Hereford, with a pneumatic-tyres 'safety' in 1893. She wears 'rational' dress, a fashion that caused an outrage at the time, but which was much more practical than the long and voluminous skirts of the period.

Opposite top: Children with tricycles at Temple Sowerby, Cumbria, in 1892. The children are 'gentry' and the machines are not juvenile models, but adult 'cast-offs'.

Opposite below: Three Worcestershire gentlemen with their machines in 1893. The machine in the middle is on pneumatic tyres and is diamond-framed, but the two on the flanks are cross-framed machines on solid tyres.

This lady's Rover cost £20 new in 1896, when this photograph was taken. The ankle-length dress was typical wear, and required such machines to have the dropped frame, leather or metal chaincase and silkcord dress-guard to accommodate it.

The Kidderminster Cycling Club enjoy an outing to Witley Court, seat of Lord Dudley, on 26 May 1897. Note the large number of ladies and their typical dress. On the extreme right is Mr Cook, Lord Dudley's Bailiff, flanked by his daughters.

The machine displayed here by Mr Sweetman, a chemist of Ludlow, Shropshire, shows that by this date (1898) the gents' bicycles were different only in detail from those of recent times

By the turn of the century very rural areas could offer a service to the cyclist. Mr Cooke, of Bredwardine in west Herefordshire, was an official CTC repairer and sold and even built cycles.

'Our Cycle Club'. This card (originally in colour) was posted to a Mrs Norman of Harrogate on 23 August 1906. The machines are American and the picture epitomises the freedom of the road.

in legal matters, the state of the roads, refreshment and accommodation facilities for cyclists on tour and many other matters concerning the well-being of cyclists in general.

The Club's winged wheel badge became familiar even in very rural districts, identifying accommodation, refreshment and repair facilities countrywide.

The pneumatic tyre had so greatly enhanced the popularity of cycling that by 1888, only five years

---

Not so Old

'How old was our departed friend?' inquired a gentleman attending a funeral in Inverness.

'Very old; very old, sir,' was the reply; 'I believe he was in his 87th year.'

'That's not very old.' exclaimed the gentleman. 'If my father had been living he'd have been 112!' – *RM*

after the change of name, membership had risen to 21,984. By 1988 this figure had increased to a staggering 60,449, a direct result of the acceptance by 'Society' of cycling as a pastime that had started in 1896. The CTC was never again to reach such membership figures. To put the growth of cycling better in perspective, one must remember that probably at least twice as many cyclists were active outside the membership of the CTC.

One of the contentious issues over which the CTC took up the cudgels was the matter of female cyclists' attire. Ankle-length skirts that the ladies customarily wore in the interests of modesty were clearly not the most suitable dress for pedalling a bicycle. Some of the bolder spirits among the lady cyclists took to what

was termed 'rational dress'... 'rational' because the dress style suited the action of cycling rather than impeding it. It revealed the legs by the use of breeches or bloomers, sometimes partially concealed by a divided skirt.

The general public was outraged by such 'immodesty' and ladies who wore this attire were subjected to verbal abuse, and even physical abuse on occasions.

A Lady Harbeton favoured 'rational dress' when cycling, and on account of this was refused

This cheerful young man's machine is towing a wickerwork trailer, whose occupant was often a lady. Since the passenger was always idle, it was hard work for the rider. The date is about 1905.

refreshments at a Surrey hotel. The CTC took up the case (Regina v Sprague in 1889), and won. Although it now behoved hoteliers and the like not to discriminate against this form of dress, it made little difference to public disapproval.

The CTC in this period did sterling work in promoting road safety and facilities of all sorts for cyclists, and also in the provision of informative and accurate road maps for cyclists. The Club laid the very sure foundations upon which the new motorists of the 20th century were to build.

The 'Society' cycle boom of the late 1890s was short-lived, as those who espoused it took up with the latest toy, the motor car. Cyclists who took up the pastime primarily because it was then the fashion were never taken seriously by dyed-in-the-wool cycle enthusiasts, but at the very least they had performed a service by rendering the pastime socially acceptable at all levels. The great degree of overproduction by the cycle makers in the boom time was followed by severe cutbacks, but also brought about a marked reduction in the average price of a good,

well made and finished machine. Only a few of the very top quality machines now sold at over £20 each. Mass production and improved materials and techniques also played an important part in reducing prices.

Early this century H G Wells wrote of his enjoyment of cycling in the pre-motor age, 'when there were no automobiles and the cyclist had a lordliness, a sense of masterful adventure, that has gone from him altogether now'. The illustrations... with not a motor car in sight, capture the spirit of this period. Although in rural areas the road surfaces had improved but little, if at all, the chance of meeting any of the new-fangled motors was slight, even at a short distance from quite large towns. There was still a sense of peace and quiet, a lack of bustle, and one must remember that the bicycle itself on its now universal pneumatic tyres travelled silently. True, its very silence could at times unnerve a restive horse or unwary pedestrian. Contrast that with the level of mechanical noise that is found today even in rural areas, and one can sympathise with the feelings of H G Wells.

Opposite above A summer tryst, perhaps. Their two bicycles lie in the hedge while she poses on the stile and he takes the photograph. The cool shade of the wood looks inviting on a hot day.

Opposite below The advantages of the pneumatic tyre were obvious and by the time of this photograph (1906) such tyres were universal on cycles. However, most rural roads did not have a tarmacadam surface and punctures were still a bugbear. The machine is a Centaur.

Overleaf A very smartly turned out young man shows off his brand new Rudge-Whitworth cycle. It has the cotterless cranks that the make favoured at the time (c.1906) and has a two-speed gear in the back hub, operated by the lever on the top tube.

Beauty From Ballast

Text and pictures by *John Hannavy*

IN the midst of some of the finest farmlands in East Lothian, at the edge of the village of East Linton, stands an eccentric group of mill buildings – a tribute not only to the ingenuity of 18th century millers, but also to the ingenuity of the master-mariners who captained the ships which helped develop Scotland's coastal shipping trade with mainland Europe.

An empty ship is an unstable ship

Preston Mill, East Lothian. Pantiles cling to the curious shapes of a mill roof, almost wrapping themselves around the conical structure. In the landscape, their colour seems entirely natural.

Culross Village. White harled walls, and pantiled roofs are synonymous with the village of the Fife coast. The basic fabric of Culross has changed to little in the past three centuries that some years ago, the National Trust for Scotland determined that it should be preserved, as an architectural time capsule. After much restoration, the village today does not disappoint.

– mariners learned that fact very early on in the history of merchant shipping, and sought ways of dealing with it. The merchantmen which carried British produce to the rest of the world, in the days of loose cargo, were often fit for only one type of produce – coal ships could carry little other than coal, grain ships could only carry grain, and there was little else which could be carried in a vessel designed for timber.

So, to avoid the risk that even a short voyage with an empty hold

Opposite **Sir David Bruce's Culross Palace. Sir David Bruce's coal mines beneath the River Forth were, probably, directly responsible for the importing of the first pantiles into Culross. It is only fitting that his own house should use them as a roofing material!**

posed to the crew – and indeed to the ship herself – ballast to weigh the ship down was carried from as long ago as the Roman times.

In the heady trading days of Britain's industrial might, ships crossed the English Channel or plied the North Sea or the Irish Sea from north to south, laden with Welsh slate, Welsh, Scottish or English coal, and Midlands iron, but often made

Crail Harbour. The 'Little Houses' at Pittenweem, Crail, and elsewhere along the East Neuk of Fife blend a variety of architectural styles and periods into the archetypal coastal village. Pantiles, modern machine made tiles, and slate roofing all add to the richness of colour on the skyline.

the return journey with little more than crushed stone or sand in the holds. Ballast banks, in the sea off many a British port, still attest to the scale of this valueless cargo.

At some point in the 16th century, some enterprising merchant hit upon a return cargo. In a number of the plates in John Slezer's *Theatricum Scotiae* published in 1693, the little stone houses along the waterfront in the Scottish village of Culross are drawn in such perfect detail that it is easy to see that over four centuries later, they have changed very little.

What makes those early illustrations so valuable, is the detail they show of the roofing materials. Some are covered in stone slabs, but the majority are covered with pantiles.

While pantiles were only just starting to appear in other parts of Britain in Slezer's day, many of the cottages and houses of Culross were already nearly a century old when the illustrations were made.

Culross grew up on the industrial exploitation of two commodities which were in considerable local abundance – taking salt from the waters of the Forth estuary, and coal from deep beneath it had been the mainstay of Culross Abbey since the early 15th century.

Both the coal and salt industries in Culross owed their considerable commercial success to Sir David Bruce who expanded and developed both the salt pans and the deep mines in the late 16th century.

His deep mine, hundreds of feet below the River Forth, was kept dry by a continuous chain of buckets driven by horse-power at the surface which sought to keep the river at bay through a drainage shaft 240ft deep – a remarkable depth for coal mining at the end of the 16th century.

Coal was not just used for heating – it provided the fuel for the fires which heated the salt pans. So coal as a fuel, and salt for preserving were both essential for 16th century life, and were often worked together.

Bruce established European trade in both products to further his own – and Culross's – prosperity. It is claimed that over a hundred tons of coal a week were being exported to Hamburg in the closing years of the 16th century from his deep-water moorings, and an unspecified amount to Holland and the other Low Countries.

Elsewhere on the east coast, the 18th century saw coal from many other mines also being exported in significant quantities – significantly from Granton and Leith, from Berwick on Tweed, and from the ports of Kent and Suffolk.

On the other side of the country, huge quantities made its way to

White Horse Close, Edinburgh. Restored in the 1960s, modern roofing, centre, seems too flat and uninteresting when compared with the rich texture of pantiles, right

Europe from Bridgewater and Watchet in Somerset, from the ports of South Wales.

On the return journey, the Dutch

Opposite **Lincoln. Many timber-framed houses, once covered with thatch, have been re-roofed in pantiles, and other interlocking variants since the early 18th century**

Opposite below **Allerford, Somerset. Bridgewater in Somerset, originally the main port of entry for pantiles, soon manufactured its own – and a variety of later lower-profile designs**

Whitby. A mixture of slate, pantile, and modern machine-made alternatives, give Whitby's skyline its distinctive warmth. Many of these tiles were probably not imported, but locally made near Hull, where their manufacture continues to this day.

coal ships carried as ballast, the cheapest commodity that Holland could export – pantiles. That ballast has come to be one of the most immediately recognisable features of those areas of Britain, and as demand for pantiles outstripped the

Saxtead Green Post Mill, Suffolk. As if to underline their early use as a roofing material for 'inferior' buildings, it is the wooden sheds and barns around this mill which are covered with pantiles. The red corrugated iron roof of the small white building is an unfortunate blot on the landscape!

ballast-carrying capacity of the coal ships, local industry quickly turned its hand to making the materials itself. Kirkcaldy, Cupar, Kincardine and Leven in Scotland, Bridgewater, Beverly and Hull in England amongst many other towns, had thriving tile-making industries throughout the 18th and 19th centuries. To this day, particularly in Humberside and North East Yorkshire, pantiles are still being made in significant quantities.

The pantile – which today we think of as an attractive decorative roofing material – was, in its early days, considered cheap and economical. Cheap, because as disposable ballast it initially had little commercial value, and economical because the way in which the tiles fitted together on the roof gave maximum cover with the minimum number of tiles.

***Opposite* Elm Hill, Norwich. Pantiles, and later less highly-profiled tiles were used extensively in Norwich and the surrounding villages, often as an alternative to thatch**

The pantile is distinct from other tiles primarily in its shape – its colour can vary considerably, from the traditional orange/red, through bright orange and even to a deep

Thorpeness Windpump, Suffolk. Not unreasonably, in an area known for its winds, the pantiles here are well helped by a liberal setting of mortar

brown. A pantile has an ogee-shaped profile, like an extended letter 'S' on its side, with one curve of much larger radius than the other. Thanks to this shape, each pantile locked easily to its neighbour on either side and, as a result, did not need the elaborate overlapping so typical of slates. Despite that interlocking

design, there was no real guarantee that a pantiled roof would be watertight, so in better quality buildings, the tiles today are bonded together with mortar ensuring a weatherproof finish.

The pantile is, traditionally, a large tile – considerably larger than many of its contemporaries, and weighing over twice as much. So, despite the greater individual weight, the reduced number of tiles per square yard of roof made for a lighter load overall. While a plain tile measures just over 10ins x 6ins, and weighs in at two and a half

Woodbridge Tidal Mill, Suffolk. The restored mill may now be roofed with a machine-made tile of later design and lower profile, but at least part of the adjacent harbour buildings still sport their pantiled roof

pounds – using metric measurements would seem to be heresy with such a traditional material, wouldn't it ? – the mighty pantile measures over 13ins x 9ins, and each weighs over five and a half pounds!

As the pantile has evolved over the centuries, it has become less curvaceous, reuslting in a flatter and less distinctively undulating roof, but the basic principle of minimum overlap and maximum coverage has not been lost. A pantiled roof, therefore, has always been both cheaper to cover, and much lighter in weight – a useful bonus when, as was often the case, pantiles were used to replace previously thatched roofs. The wooden framework on to which the thatch had been applied might not have supported stone, slate, or plain tiles but would certainly support the lighter covering of pantiles.

And the pantile, traditionally, had a peg or 'nib' at the top, so that it could be hung from a roof batten or lath – in its dry-hung form, it was not entirely unknown for pantiled roofs to lift up, despite their weight, and blow away at the height of winter gales.

Despite their apparent imperma-nence, pantiled roofs have come to be synonymous with Somerset, the Yorkshire and Northumberland coasts, and parts of the east coast of Scotland – particuarly Fife and the Forth estuary.

It is their irregularity, their undu-lation, and their variety of colour which is their attraction – always hand made, pantiles, thankfully, never have that smooth and repeti-tive mechanical symmetry of their machine-made successors. Indeed, today's pantiles are still hand made, ensuring that they blend easily and satisfyingly into restored roofs, retaining a rich textural quality which is all their own. That cheapest of materials once used to ballast coal ships has turned into one of British architecture's most endearing and enduring eccentricities.

Lord Iveagh's Treasure

At Elveden Hall, Suffolk, May 1984, there was a grand sale which attract-ed people from all over the country and even further afield. Only the older of the locals, and a few visiting Americans knew of the Hall's wartime his-tory, but even they were surprised to see old signs still on the walls in some rooms and outbuildings, left over from WW2.

The house had been the HQ of the 3rd Air Division of the 8th USAAF. It was this which attracted a few of the Americans, some of whom had been stationed there. This unit controlled most of the American bases in East Anglia and planned the raids into nazi Germany they were engaged upon. From this house went the directions for the daylight raids, moni-tored them, logged and counted them as they returned. It was their task too to record those who did not come back and inform their next of kin.

A great many of the old signs remained – do they still? – recalling old scenes and nostalgic memories. One of the rooms still carried on its door the name of Lt Col Spencer who became a four star general after the war.

A few, remembering, might have asked between the bids, for a moment's silence, but no-one did, most were too young to realise why. – *Eunice Wilson*

Lambs'-Tail Pie and Strawberries

Heather Wood

The following extracts are from Tales of the Old Countrywomen by Brian P Martin and Tales of the Old Horsemen by Jennifer Davies, published by David & Charles, Brunel House, Newton Abbot, Devon TQ12 4PU

ALTHOUGH farming generally has changed dramatically since World War 2, some things remain as important as ever. The new breed of highly educated agro-businessman may crop a better return on investments, yet never experience the real job satisfac-

tion which his forebears enjoyed. Traditional farming should not be the plaything of profiteers, but rather an entire way of life based on subsistence and sustainable natural resources, and it is the man or woman who has true empathy with the seasons and animals who will reap the greatest rewards. Such a person is Heather Wood (nee Thompson) who, among many other things, has cared for sheep for over half a century.

While the tycoon may regard a flock of sheep as no more than x num-

The cover illustration for
Tales of the Old Countrywomen is by John Paley and Alex Webb-Peploe

ber of meat and wool units, to Heather every animal is an individual requiring year-round attention.

A very modest and gentle lady, as befits the good shepherdess, Heather has always been close to the land and livestock, and immersed in Cotswold life. She was born at Elm Bank Farm, Cold Aston, Gloucestershire on 16 October 1935, and later moved to neighbouring Camp Farm, both places being run by her father. And when she married Nolan, in 1959, she moved only about fifteen miles away, to Sugarswell Farm, a mile or two outside Hook Norton, where her husband is still a tenant. There, among the north Oxfordshire hills, sheep and warm stone cottages have characterised the countryside since the Middle Ages.

As lambing time approaches, Heather becomes very single-minded:

'You have to keep looking all the time for problems such as prolapsing, which is very common. I never go out at lambing and I don't like visitors. We have a multi-purpose shed here, and that's cleared to accommodate the ewes: even my husband's vintage tractors go out!

'All our ewes are brought inside

every night, but with bigger flocks, where lambing is over a longer period, some farmers use different colour raddle so that they know when each ewe is going to lamb and look after it accordingly. (Raddle, reddle or ruddle is a coloured material – often red ochre – applied to the chest of the ram so that those ewes which have been mated are marked). One extraordinary thing that's always impressed me is how many of our ewes know their own spot in the barn.

'After lambing, each ewe and her offspring are put into individual hurdle pens for a couple of days, to make sure they are suckling and feeding well before they go out.'

Heather has become very attached to some of her sheepdogs. She told me about two in particular:

'This is "Trim", who's twelve years old and came from a neighbour. At first she'd round up the ducks but not the sheep, so she had to go away with another shepherd for eight weeks. She's trained to the voice because I never could whistle, unlike my Dad. But her sight's not too good now. Sometimes, when I'm in the kitchen and look out I can see her following my scent where I've been to the washing line, and she never set-

Special Book Offer

Tales from the Countryside

A fascinating collection of reminiscences and stories from a wide range of rural characters, recording a way of life that is rapidly disappearing.

Tales of the Old Horsemen
Jennifer Davies

This wonderful book gathers the stories of people who have spent their lives working with horses in varied situations, from army horsemen in the days of the British Cavalry, to keepers of working farm horses, to the man who was the Queen's head coachman for almost a quarter of a century.

Published Price £17.99
Special Offer Price With Author's Signature £15.99

Tales of the Old Countywomen
Brian P. Martin

Country life through the eyes of countrywomen, this fascinating book recounts tales from a broad range of women, including an independent shepherdess, the supportive wife of a gamekeeper and a high-born lady with an entourage of servants.

Published Price £17.99
Special Offer Price With Author's Signature £15.99

To order, call the David & Charles Credit Card Hotline on (01626) 334555 and quote code N006. Postage and packing is free in the UK mainland. Alternatively, send your order with a cheque to David & Charles Direct, PO Box 6, Newton Abbot, Devon TQ12 2DW.

tles if I'm away. When she retires, I think I'll retire too.

'Before Trim I had Lassie – but perhaps Glen was the most remarkable dog our family ever had. He was blind when we had him, but he was a clever dog and worked the sheep well: he knew all the gaps in the hedges and had no problem bringing the sheep down the hill when required. He loved cars and our old Ford was the only place where you could shut him up. And you only ever tied him up once – there's the scars on my arm to prove it!

'He also took a huge hunk out of my sister Rita's leg because she got down-wind of the sheep. He'd round up everything, even the hens.

'One day Glen went missing and we drove all over the fields in the Ford Ten calling his name, into the woods and along the hedgerows. Then we came to this old, dry well, one of many dug in the Cotswolds in search of water, and we hardly dared peer in. But there he was, miraculously clinging to a piece of wood jutting out the side.

'We fetched a long ladder from the barn and gently lowered it into the well, but this was greeted by snarls and desperate growls because Glen couldn't see what was happening. So father gently coaxed and whistled and talked to him and we edged the ladder as close to him as possible. After a while, Glen put out a tentative paw, felt the hardness of the ladder, and then wrapped his front legs around a bottom rung, allowing us to pull him up, clinging on for dear life. It was a wonderful moment when he came to the surface.'

Heather has also had some very unusual pets...

'On Dad's farm I had a lamb called Jill, which never left my side. Even when I went ploughing with the tractor she would always run along in front of the wheel. Then one day we had to go to my sister's school sports day and Jill was shut in. But as soon as we moved off she got out and started following us, and this happened several times so we gave up and took her with us in the car. But when we were at the sports field she had to stay inside the vehicle and wait for us. There were a few surprised faces around! One day she got into the garden and ate everything, so then Dad insisted that she had to go.

'I also had a pig, a large white called Emily. When she was young she got to like sucking milk from a lamb's bottle, and she never forgot this. Even when she was full grown she'd sit on her haunches just like a dog and wait for me to give her a bottle!'

Country life has certainly changed a great deal since Heather arrived at Sugarswell Farm. On the very day the Woods moved in as they were taking the window out to get the bed in, the grocer turned up to take his first order!

Yet while country folk generally must now travel long distances to towns in order to shop relatively cheaply, townsfolk are eager to get out into the countryside to pick fruit and vegetables such as Heather's strawberries. 'But I don't think it's a bargain they are after,' said Heather, 'it's more the space and fresh air they want.'

A Very Determined Lady

Jeanne Robinson

FROM parachutists to poachers, from bureaucrats to bunglers, anyone uninvited who has ever dared put even an unwelcome toe on Jeanne Robinson's land has risked life and limb. When Germans dropped in while practising for the invasion, Jeanne was ready with her Great War revolver and hand grenade, although she does not admit to 'bagging' any. And other intruders have found themselves staring down the barrels of her shotgun. Yet here is no hill-billy, no rustic result of centuries of local in-breeding. On the contrary, Jeanne had a very privileged and sophisticated upbringing, and even went to finishing school in Vienna. No, it was the circumstances of her birth which made her such a resourceful lady, one of great independence who would stop at almost nothing to protect the land she loves.

Here she describes what made her so determined:

'I was born in hospital, in Belgravia, on 3 June 1919. My mother came from a prominent Cornish family – she and her sisters were known as "the five beauties of Lostwithiel", and their father was county surveyor – and my father was an Australian army captain. But my parents were not married, so mother had to be rid of me. My grandparents, the Knights, disowned me too: they gave the midwife just £10 for a pram and said they never wanted to see me again. And later, at school, the other children would say, "she hasn't got a mother". But that's what made me such a fighter.

'This was an isolated part of the country then, and remained quite unspoilt into the 1960s. I specially loved the river, and it was so peaceful walking on the marsh, with only the birdsongs and wind to accompany you. But more than anything to me, Bradwell meant swimming and sailing. When I was fourteen I swam over two miles across the Blackwater to West Mersea, to get an ice-cream. And when I was fifteen Mummy gave me a fifteen-footer – and I always kept a dagger in my waistband in case I capsized and had to cut myself free.

'Trusses Cottage was very old, with an earth closet, paraffin lamps and water from a pump – complete with worms. We had a ghost, too: one night I woke up with a start and something went straight through the window; but perhaps that comes through being Cornish.

'The village was very closed then, and almost everybody had lived there for ages. Usually you had to have three generations in the churchyard before you were regarded as local, but

Jeanne in 1933 – living life in the fast lane

the natives were friendly towards us and admired Mummy's midwifery. Everybody had nicknames in Essex – and most still do – and very often you don't even know someone's real name.

'We used to travel down in a car with solid tyres, but the roads were very bad so when pneumatics arrived we were always getting punctures; but then I discovered that if I stood on the bank and lifted my skirt I soon got help!

'This area was mostly sheep country then, but Jack Parker grew enormous fields of daffodils – a lovely sight – for the bulbs, which he would send off to market aboard his old Thames sailing barges. Although the railway had come down to Southminster in 1886, barges were still widely used to take hay and straw round to London, and to bring back the muck from dairy cowsheds to spread on the fields. Also, the barges were good because many roads

remained rough up to the last war. I've still got a barge hard – a little dock – on my farm.

'In those days of rationing, all the farmers had to sell their stock to the government, and even if you kept more than a few hens you had to sell the eggs to the Ministry. It was my job to count what was brought in, to put the animals in the pens for assessment by the grading officer, and to write out the payment cheques. If a farmer filled in a form to say he was bringing in twenty sheep and he brought in twenty-one, then one had to go back which didn't go down very well. Mine wasn't a reserved occupation for women, and in fact there was only one other woman doing this in the whole country – halfway up some Welsh mountain – but they let me carry on.

'They were dirty old men in the market, and they liked me to wear a skirt so they could see the lace and colour of my knickers when I bent over the pig pen; so mostly I obliged!

'They were all tight as newts after about half a bottle of whisky each – but they were gentlemen, too, and always took their caps off to me.'

On marrying Tom, Jeanne soon became involved in everyday work on the 400-acre Stamford's Farm, which to this day remains a remarkable oasis of yesteryear. Apart from changes due to acts of God, the fields, boundaries, hedgerows and marshes remain much the same as they were in a record of 1685, and the well maintained house, with its white-painted weather-boarding and black-framed windows, goes back to 1400 or earlier. The only modern addition is the sunroom, which has become a real refuge for Jeanne since she had a stroke in 1992. Here she can sit in some comfort to do the *Daily Telegraph* crossword and to ·grapple with the ever-increasing paperwork involved in running a farm; and more importantly, she can look out over

her delightful garden and beyond to the saltmarshes which she has loved for so long.

It was here that we sat, reflecting on Jeanne's very full life, occasionally interrupted by farming associates and telephone calls from 'the nature people' negotiating over the new designation of her marshes as environmentally sensitive, the whole of which area was being classified as a Site of Special Scientific Interest. Indeed, Jeanne is most anxious not only to preserve the rich saltmarsh ecosystem, but also to return arable acres to grass, so that the entire farm will be for grazing only and thereby conservation-friendly. She told me that she and Tom never had any interest in farming for big profits, only for the good of the land – and perhaps for her young grandson if he wants to take over.

Hard work in the 1950s: women farm workers pulling up individual brussels sprout plants, grown from seed planted with a hand-pushed drill

A Royal Coachman

Arthur Showell

A cobbled forecourt and rainwater pipes embossed with the date 1570 confirm the venerability of the place in which Arthur and Yvonne Showell live. The complex once formed the stables and coachhouses of one of the royal palaces; it still is, in fact, part of that palace, but nowadays the coach-houses are garages and the stables and grooms' quarters are comfortable flats.

Yvonne is a kind, hospitable person. She is quietly proud of Arthur's achievements in life and keeps a book of newspaper cuttings which mark occasions in his career. Arthur's life with horses deserves recording. It culminated in his becoming HM the Queen's head coachman at Buckingham Palace Mews. He held this post for 23 years before he and Yvonne retired to their flat by the Thames.

Arthur is compact in build. When he talks, his rounded features are bright with enthusiasm and he laughs cheerfully. However, it is obvious that he can stand his ground when he feels it is needed.

Both Arthur and Yvonne are Jersey born and bred, and they still visit and love the island. Jersey acknowledges Arthur too, for not so long ago when their Philatelic Bureau published a stamp to honour a royal occasion, they used a photograph of Arthur on its presentation pack: it shows him in full livery driving the Queen in the Ivory Phaeton to the ceremony of Trooping the Colour. Arthur describes his early history thus:

'I was born in 1926. My parents never had any money and there was no such thing as the Pony Club, so because I loved horses, I used to go round all the local stables in St Helier just to get as much as I could of what in those days they called cartage. They'd let you drive the horses and I used to learn a lot from watching them. For example, the way they loaded their vehicles. They'd put two tons of coal or sand or gravel from the sea on a two-wheeled vehicle. It had to be balanced correctly so there wasn't too much weight on the horse's back. As the loaded cart approached a hill the carter would usually stand on the shafts; that stopped the shafts going up in the air when the horse climbed the hill and also kept the weight on its back. Some people would say "Look at that lazy so-and-so making the horse pull him up the hill". They didn't realise that he'd walked a couple of miles, just to make sure that there wasn't too much weight on the horse's back during the journey.

'I'd help take the horses down to the beach on a Sunday morning, too. If the tide was right, the carters would get me to jump on their horses' backs and take them into the sea and swim them. The carters would each bring an old dandy brush with them and when their horse came out, brush all the feather on its legs and give each one a good clean up because they used to think that salt water was a good remedy. Nowadays people turn hosepipes on their horses' legs for tendons and suchlike, but in those days we took them into the sea.

'I spent a lot of time with a firm called Pitchers. They used to have horses what we called vanners which were a cross between a riding horse and a draught horse and which could be put into a four-wheeled van for haulage. They also had a livery yard with about twenty horses of all kinds, and they owned a bus company which did island trips. One of their vehicles was a sixteen-seater horse-drawn car called a "Tantivy".'

Arthur was thirteen when the war broke out. He describes the effect on Jersey when the Germans first

Tales of the
OLD
HORSEMEN

JENNIFER DAVIES

moved in to occupy it: 'The island was in full swing with plenty of food in the shops, and when the German troops arrived and saw so much stuff they bought it all up quickly and sent it back to Germany. Well, it wasn't long before the shops were empty. Pitchers had a shop down in the Parade and they were sensible because before it was too late, they shut shop and took everything home. Put it under the floorboards.'

Pitchers and other haulage firms actually benefited from the German occupation, because with petrol being short, horse-drawn vehicles were in demand. As Arthur recalls:

'Everybody started looking for landaus or any kind of horse-drawn carriage that was laid up in the manors around the island; there was quite a lot of carriages to be got hold of. Old Boss Pitcher was a bit shrewd and got himself a variety of vehicles like landaus, barouches, wagonettes, funeral carriages, horse hearses, more coaches and vans and a useful vehicle called a brougham, and went into the cabbing business. People could ring up for a carriage and pair or a single horse to go somewhere. Riding for pleasure completely stopped. The only time you got a ride in those days was when you jumped up and rode bareback to the blacksmith's shop.

One of the bad things was that there wasn't much food for the horses. You couldn't get a lot of oats, and although it was grown locally, hay went up to £40 a ton. That doesn't sound much today, but in those days wages were 30s (£1.50p) and £2, so there's the difference. Horses were in such poor condition their collars had to be small so that they fitted around their shoulders. You had to force these collars over the horse's head - in fact you tried to open them up by putting them on your knee and pulling them, and some people would

A Jersey farmer leads his horse on to the weighbridge

put them on the floor and push down from the pointed end. It was always a struggle to get the collar on, but I thought that was natural, I just thought, well, the horse had got a big head and that's it. It was only after the war that I learnt different - in fact, when I went to work in Hampshire for Sir Dymoke White. His horses were in such good condition and their necks so big but the collars went easily over the heads and correctly fitted the shoulders. It was quite an eye-opener to me.

'We used to mix molasses with the horses' food, a sweet substance like black treacle, and were often so hungry we'd eat a bit ourselves! Mangolds was another horse food - a root similar to a swede - and the prickly shrub with a yellow bloom called gorse. We called that furze or fuzz. We'd bundle it up and put some risers on the van to cope with the high load. We put it through the chaff cutter, but because of the spikes on it we used to wear a pair of thick gloves and use a stick or some-

thing to get it through. Some of the heavy horses had a moustache on the upper lip and people used to say: "He's a good fuzz eater", because the moustache would protect him!' Arthur chuckles at this memory. Still considering gorse, he adds: 'Horses sometimes suffer from lampas, a swelling of the gums in the upper jaw. But it was said that horses fed on gorse never had it - and gorse was a good treatment for it, too. I also found out in later years that if you had a horse with severe colic and were lucky enough to have it recover, it would of course still be out of sorts and would take a long time to get eating again. However, if you got a nice bundle of gorse and strung it up in the corner of the stable, then a horse would somehow get some comfort from it and start picking away at it.'

Going back to their wartime days in Jersey, Yvonne describes the household food they had: 'We were existing on swedes, a few potatoes, but mainly swedes. My grandmother could get Jersey milk, so she used to bring it to the boil and then skim off the cream and make butter.'

A Good Scottish Vet

The story goes that once Sir Walter Scott was spending the night at a Scottish border inn and while having a crack with a local worthy who was also a veterinary surgeon, he asked the vet if he confined his practice to animals. The old man admitted he was often called in to treat strangers who might have fallen ill. When Sir Walter Scott heard some of the remedies carried out by the old-horse doctor, he remarked that some of the drugs mentioned were quite dangerous and had the vet seen any serious consequences through administering them? 'Oh, aye,' replied the old chap; 'twa or three ha'e dee'd, but they were English, and it'll tak' a lang time before we make up for Flodden.' – *R.M.*

Living off the fat of the land

EACH era has its own chosen route to riches. In the late 1940s and early 1950s, the thing to be was a butcher. Everyone knew it was the butcher who was coining it, spending liberally yet afraid to spend too much lest the game was totally given away.

Whoever invented the way the meat ration worked, and prolonged rationing until well into the 1950s, must have wished to favour butchers. The ration was by price. So if you were entitled as a family to say 3s 9d worth of joint, if the butcher winked at you while saying it was four shillings and a halfpenny, you thought (or at least wondered about) getting a bit more than you should.

So scarce was meat, that nobody could afford to argue with the butcher even when useless fat was left on a joint. Demand your rights and you would surely miss out on those other scarce but unrationed things like suet and sausages. Placed in such a tempting position, few butchers could resist rounding up (and then adding an old halfpenny to give conviction) – and to avoid having to put a finger on the scales many hit on the idea of a few percentage points of adjustment to the scale or use of an inconspicuous extra weight. Indeed, it was said that the government so suspected butchers to cheat that an absolutely honest one would really struggle.

So why do we have nostalgic memories of our weekend visit to the butcher? Possibly because it was a great social meeting place. Queues usually began outside the shop and you were sure to bump into someone you knew. Possibly also because we knew we were taking a weekly gamble and if we were young wondered how mum would react to our purchase this week. Pretty girls always had the advantage over boys, but well-spoken respectable lads pleading that an aunt was coming to Sunday lunch could also do well. It sure makes today's supermarket shopping seem dull.

Beastly Deception

A remarkable case once came before the Sheriff of Perthshire. A farmer from Auchterarder had sold a cow to a man from Perth and the buyer summoned the farmer in the order to recover damages, because he'd been given false information about the cow. "I asked him if she was a good milker," said the plaintiff. "And what was his reply?" asked the Sheriff. "He said, she'll astonish you! I took her home, but she has not a single drop of milk." "Well", said the Sheriff, "she has." He then ordered the case to be dismissed. – *R.M.*

RECORDED MEMORIES

Christmas Pre-War

A Woollen Mill in the Cotswolds

UP until World War 2, the workers at Longfords woollen mill, near Nailsworth in the South Cotswolds, used to have regular Christmas outings to the theatre. Sylvia Raines described them:

'We used to put threepence a week, each of us, and at Christmas, we used to go to the pantomime at Bristol. We had taxis to go in, and it was a Mr Mortimer from up Forest Green way that ran the taxis. We used to leave work early – two or three taxis would come up to the factory gates, and we'd all troop out – we'd take our best bib and tucker, sort of thing, and put it on. And we'd go to Bristol, we'd go and have a plaice and chips or something first at one of the restaurants, and then go into the – I think it was the Prince's – Theatre in the centre of Bristol to see the pantomime. Oh, we thoroughly enjoyed that, it was something that people could do, like that: these days someone would get in a car or something and go up to London, but you just couldn't do it in those days.

And I remember one time: we were seeing Red Riding Hood, and there was an older lady that did come with us. It had got to the part where the wolf was trying to catch Red Riding Hood in the forest, and all was quiet. The wolf grabbed hold of Red Riding Hood, and this old lady stood up in her seat, and she said, "Oh the devil got her!" – Everybody roared with laughter!...'

A Hard Winter at Longfords

WINTERS often seem to have been colder when we were young, but Sylvia Raines could remember when the Lake at Longfords Mill, where she worked - a lake covering 12 or 13 acres, and normally about 26ft deep – actually froze over:

'I remember the year we had a dreadful winter; everything froze solid, and the lake itself actually froze – it's unbelievable really, to think that all that running water could freeze. And there were men, women, youngsters and all, we actually walked out on that lake. When I think of it today, it makes my blood go cold, it does really! – to think we were out on it, because it's quite a depth, that lake. And there's one fellow in Hampton now, he was there, working as a lad, and he actually walked from one side of that lake to the other. That lake was frozen solid!...'

Sylvia Raines was talking to Jacqueline Sarsby

Death to Rural Railways

David St John Thomas

IN the 1950s and 1960s, British Railways finally realised they could not continue essentially pre-war policies for ever and had to improve main lines on the one hand and prune the rural systems on the other.

Whether you wanted a better service to London, relied on trains to bring your visitors, or were horrified at the thought of the line on which you went to school being closed, railways were news. Just about everyone cared, as indeed they should have done since in those days punctual running had to be relied upon to bring the post and morning newspapers and take milk, fruit and vegetables to up-country markets. More than that, the resorts which grew most rapidly in the formative years after the war were those with good train services (no major West Country resort was ever established off the network), and where the new wave of retirees decided to live was in most cases influenced by how quickly they could get back to civilisation when the need occurred, even if that was usually more psychological than practical.

In the 1950s most trains were steam hauled and the earliest Plymouth and Torbay folk could get to London was 12.15pm, while a day trip from Cornwall was impractical since the first day-time train did not reach the capital before the last one had set out on the return journey. Only a couple of Light Railways had been closed before the war, and for nearly all the 1950s Cornwall had seen only four passenger-station closures. At rural centres such as Halwill Junction (the community named after the station) cattle were still carried on a prodigious scale, and over the gradients on the southern tips of Dartmoor the Western Region's steam freights had to be given extra banking power on the way up and have the brakes of individual trucks applied by hand at a special stop before the descent.

As far as branch line closures were concerned, possibly nothing in their history has so united many country towns and villages than the threat to their railway. The arguments still have a familiar ring: British Railways had tried neither to attract business nor make economies that were glaringly obvious; without trains, local commerce would suffer;

how would anyone be able to travel when roads were closed by snow?

The closure process began with the publication of a 'Public Announcement', proposing closure, listing alternative arrangements, and stating to whom objections could be made. The local Transport Users Consultative Committee (TUCC) had to decide between inconvenience, allowable in the cause of economy and progress, and hardship which was not. That was its sole brief, evidence about BR's poor performance, or even how a single train might do the work of three and save on signalling as well as locomotive and carriage costs, was out of order. BR officials realised their record was awful, but generally blamed someone else internally, quarrels between the traffic and engineering sides absorbing much energy that should have been used more constructively to attract business and tailor services and costs.

The waste was often prodigious, passengers frequently costing ten times as much as they paid in fares, and on freight-only branches costs equalling £1 per ton per mile carried. Slight adjustments crying out to be made were ignored; on one line a slight timetable adjustment taking advantage of the fact that for decades a train stood empty for 90 minutes between turns, since its use during that period had been cancelled in the 1930s, could have eliminated another working and enabled the closure of a signalbox manned two turns unnecessarily even during the war years. But, no, lines were sometimes relaid up to the time of their closure, and at least one station was being painted while another received a new fireplace as the last train called.

Only when a divisional set up replaced the traditional district one (and in the West Country's case former Western and Southern lines were amalgamated) did common

Overleaf **Some lines were closed even pre-war, and many others followed in the 1950s before Beeching's era. Final days of operation meant longer trains to accommodate those taking a last (and often their only) trip along a picturesque route. On 9 June 1955, two trains with more than their usual carriages pass at the loop on the single-track Teign Valley line at Christow. The fireman walking to the water column to replenish his engine is Bob Wise, later for many year's the writer's gardener.**

Below **Two engines were needed to haul the six carriages up to Princetown on the last day of service across the highest Dartmoor branch**

SUBSCRIPTION AND ENROLMENT FORM

FOR ALL SUBSCRIBERS AND MEMBERS

Mr/Mrs/Miss ....

Please use CAPITAL LETTERS

Address ....

....

.... Postcode ....

I would like to pay by: (Please tick one box only but be sure to give your full details)

☐ **A. DEBIT/CREDIT CARD** (Switch/Delta/Electron, Visa, Access/Mastercard or Amex)

I authorise you to debit my debit/credit card with the annual subscription on receipt and annually thereafter on the same date unless cancelled by me.

1. Please tick box ☐ Switch/Delta/Electron   ☐ Visa   ☐ Access/Mastercard   ☐ Amex

2. Card No ☐☐☐☐☐☐☐☐☐☐☐☐☐☐☐☐☐☐☐

3. Expiry date ☐☐ — ☐☐

4. Signed .... Date ....

☐ **B. DIRECT DEBIT**

Payment instruction to Bank/Building Society Originator's Identification No: 930895

1. To the Manager ....

....Bank/Building Society

2. Account in the Name of ....

3. Account No ☐☐☐☐☐☐☐.☐☐   Sort code ☐☐ — ☐☐ — ☐☐

4. Instruction to Bank/Building Society

Please pay The Countrylover's Club Direct Debits from the account detailed on this Instruction subject to the safeguards assured by The Direct Debit Guarantee.

5. Signed .... Date ....

☐ **C. CASH**   Cheques should be made payable in sterling to COUNTRY ORIGINS

SUBSCRIPTION TO COUNTRY ORIGINS

		UK	Europe	ROW
A/B	☐ Country Origins & Calendar by Debit/Credit Card or Direct Debit	£14.20	£17.75	£21.40
C	☐ Country Origins & Calendar by cash	£15.75	£19.70	£23.75

You May Of Course Cancel At Any Time

Return completed form to: COUNTRY ORIGINS, PO Box 4, Nairn IV12 4HU

CO1097

TO YOUR NEWSAGENT
Please place a regular order for the quarterly *Country Origins*.
Next issue on sale 13 March 1998.

Name ....

Address ....

.... Postcode ....

Recommend a Friend...
Know Someone Who Would Benefit From COUNTRY ORIGINS?

Just think of all your friends who are interested in yesterday's countryside and its people. Now send us their names... we will send them details of COUNTRY ORIGINS (without mentioning your name) – and each time one of them becomes a subscriber you will receive a free copy of COUNTRY ORIGINS.

Please send details of COUNTRY ORIGINS to:
(Names and addresses in CAPITALS please)

Name ....

Address ....

....

....

....

.... Postcode ....

Name ....

Address ....

....

....

.... Postcode ....

Name ....

Address ....

....

....

.... Postcode ....

(Any further names and address may be written on a separate piece of paper and attached to this form)

MY OWN DETAILS ARE:

Subscription No ....

Name ....

Address ....

....

....

.... Postcode ....

To: COUNTRY ORIGINS, PO BOX 4, NAIRN IV12 4HU   CO1097

sense belatedly take root, and by then it was too late to save most lines.

So in most cases the local TUCC rubber stamped closure, ruling there would be no hardship, and where they did not they were generally over-ruled by the national TUCC or the Minister of Transport who had the last word, or their recommendation of only temporary closure until a cheaper diesel unit became available was simply ignored after dieselisation. So having been initially postponed, the closure happened, 'as and from' the first day on which there would have been trains, always a Monday, which meant that in the case of lines without a Sunday service (as most were at least by then) the last trains ran on Saturday.

'Funerals' became almost sporting events, attracting a large crowd of enthusiasts who compared notes about previous burials and bought souvenir tickets and even quietly removed anything that could be carried away. Of course the locals were also there and many of both categories were taking their first as well as last trip over the line, and hardly any were indeed regular users. In a few cases an old lady or gent were taking their second-ever ride, the first having been on opening day, while others recalled how their parents or grandparents had been on the first train. Sometimes local traders who affectionately remembered the days their businesses depended on the line, and people who had gone by school train in their youth and brought along their kids to show them what it used to be like, added a touch of useful copy.

The last trains were often late into the evening, noisy and crowded, those who really wanted to experience yesteryear having had to travel weeks earlier before the final surge of business. Sometimes BR encouraged last-minute support; in others they stupidly ran the very last train empty. 'It is advertised to be empty and if you travel by it it won't be,' said by a guard almost literally pushing away would-be passengers, made one splendid Monday morning headline. Alas, he was so ridiculed in following weeks that he became ill; officials responsible for the silly decision and railway police kept away, though the refreshment room at the station concerned (Helston in Cornwall) had an extension to allow people to drink to its demise. In Ireland, things became so embarrassing that CIE quietly withdrew trains days before the advertised date.

Some of the most famous of the railway funerals were those of erstwhile secondary main lines, such as that of the Waverley route from Edinburgh to Carlisle, where their last trains were delayed by direct action. Often the final train, displaying a wreath and its engine whistling while fog signals were detonated beneath it, ran so late as to be into the day after it should have ceased. On the Plymouth-Launceston line, the locomotives of all three last trains had to drop their fires as they became snowbound. Cut off by a blizzard on Dartmoor, that was an event this reporter covered by numerous telephone calls with stations along the route hours after the staff were supposed to have left for good.

A LOOK AT A TRADE

The Lace Maker

The view of the lace maker has, more than most, changed over time. In 1905 it was reported as a job that old ladies used to do, while at earlier times it was a life long career involving people from aged four or five until old age. Although to a small extent lace making would have taken place throughout the UK, the majority of lace making took place in two areas, the first an area around Honiton in Devon covering east and north Devon, and the second, much larger area, covering most of Northamptonshire, Bedfordshire, Buckinghamshire, and the parts of Oxfordshire and Huntingdonshire that joined this block.

Lace making in these areas was a major cottage industry affecting the lives of the majority of the female population of the countryside and was at its peak in the 1850s. The censuses of 1851 to 1871 recorded the working pattern of females in detail and although it would have underestimated the numbers due to part time workers being often overlooked, the proportion of the workforce involved is apparent, with in 1851 in Buckinghamshire 10,487 pillow lace makers while 2,922 straw platters, 1,066 farm servants, 106 farm labourers and twelve glovers are recorded in the county. Of these lace makers 621 were aged between five and nine and

1,424 between ten and fourteen. Northamptonshire had 10,322 female lace makers including 754 between five and nine and 2,124 between 10 and fourteen, Bedfordshire 5,734, Devon 5,478, compared with counties further from the lace making centres such as Essex with 382 and Somerset with 417. Although by this time there were lace making machines these could not compare in quality terms with the pillow lace makers and could not undertake some types of lace making. Lace making got a boost from the Great Exhibition of 1851 but was slowly killed off by regulation in the form of factories and workshop regulations and the various measures to stop children working and required school attendance.

A large percentage of the documentation available to us today relates to the use of children, and as much of it was created by those who were campaigning to stop or control child labour, it perhaps does not offer a neutral view of the situation. We do however see that in lace making areas, lace schools were common. In 1835 Newport Pagnell in Buckinghamshire had fifteen lace schools between them accounting for 220 girls. Lace schools generally provided no education but concentrated on teaching lace making skills and production.

Skills were thought best acquired at an early age and some accounts tell of four year olds starting by spending half days. Accounts vary slightly but it would appear that most of these schools were small containing less than ten children, and would be a small room on the back of a cottage. Small rooms with blocked up chimneys were chosen. No fires were allowed as it effected the quality of the lace, and therefore to be possible to work in winter, a number of bodies were required in a small space to generate enough heat. Some accounts tell of girls bringing pots with lids containing embers or charcoal to put on the ground under their skirts to provide some heat. In some areas and for some parts of the year, lace making was done outside when possible.

The child would start by doing some simple parts and then progress. In most areas there was no charge for attending lace schools but the person running it would initially keep all the work produced, and as the person progressed or got older would either pay them something for the work produced or allow them to keep a part of it. In some cases the parents supplied or paid for the materials and paid a small fee and had the lace

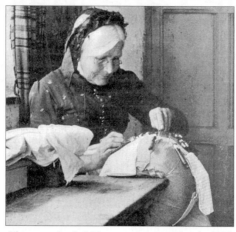

Photograph of old lace maker working in 1905

produced. Although discipline was strict with arms and necks having to be left uncovered to allow punishments to be regularly given, most accounts show that girls preferred to work as a group even when they improved their skills, rather than be moaned at by their mothers if they worked at home. Some accounts also tell of special rhymes and other bits of fun such as locking out the mistress when she left the room. The hours varied with the season, and demand for lace. Generally hours were longer in the summer, in most areas children from twelve to sixteen worked from 6am to 8pm, but in some areas until 10pm. In winter a special type of table was used which held a single candle and had a number of small poles in which glass orbs a little like upside down small jam jars could be held. These acted a little like magnifying glasses and concentrated the light from the candle to specific places, and allowed a number of people to get the effects of a single candle. To pass the hours they were encouraged to recite lace tells, often elaborate tales about the supernatural or macabre tales of violent deaths. Some were rhymes about lace making or the number and pattern of pins used in different designs. Races were held and other methods used to encourage faster work and increased dexterity.

Lace is not a form of weaving, and is produced by plaiting or twisting a number of strands of cotton or silk while controlling the shape using a pattern of pins. The basic requirement is for a pillow stuffed hard with straw, pins and a number of bobbins about the size of pencils made of wood, bone or ivory. The pillow and bobbin techniques are said to have originated in Germany in 1575, but earlier forms using netting and needles goes back to early times with Latin authors referring to it as phyrygian art. Buckinghamshire lace would appear to have usually been complete pieces with patterns, while Devon lace was constructed by creating small pieces representing leaves and other recognisable items and connecting these together with lace pieces, sewing or by putting the small parts on a net. Workers would buy the materials from a dealer and sell back the completed work, or pieces. Often the dealer would employ older girls to assemble these into finished products. Payment in Devon used the truck system, where the dealer also had a shop or store and either paid directly in goods or allowed payments to be only spent in the store. In order to work, the family had to buy all its items from the store and truck purchases were usually charged at a higher rate than normal purchases, for example a pound of white sugar was 6.5d but 8d to truck workers. Items purchased were also limited both to specific times and by volume so as to prevent people from purchasing items for resale even at a loss. This was done so as to prevent the workers from creating cash so that they could become independent, and often meant that work also had to be done in a lace workshop. Sometimes a group of girls would club together and in their own time make a collar between them to sell. But if found out they would lose their place in the lace shop and not be able to work again in that area.

The lace maker's cushion was often perched on a three legged stool, but small children often unable to lift it, had to bend over the cushion, causing some medical problems in later life.

Working conditions in schools and workshops were not good, being poorly lit, having no ventilation and suffered from sanitary and other problems. However, it was a form of employment that had very many older people still employed, and a few years later, when the schools had closed and industrial legislation closed down the industry, it was remembered for its employment of elderly people, although to gain the speed and dexterity they would have all started at a young age.

Although the hours were long, discipline strict, and payment methods often unfair, it has to be viewed in comparison with other activities of the time such as chimney boys. Used to clean chimneys, the mudlarks in the London Thames, child prostitutes and children in the mines. Looked at in this light perhaps we can see why it was so popular in the areas where the work was available.

COMPETITIONS

STILL TIME TO ENTER

Annual Country Story Competition

First prize:
A Sharp Font Writer FW-760 plus £100 plus a silver cup

Since advertising this competition in the Summer 1997 issue we are happy to announce that we have improved the prize and the winner will now receive £100 plus a Sharp Font Writer FW-760, the user friendly word-processor. On top of that, the winner gets to hold the prestigious Country Silver Cup for one year.

So what do you have to do to win. Every year *Country Origins*, in association with its sister title *Writing Magazine*, runs a competition for stories about the countryside. Entries can be about any aspect of the country scene – country people, places or happenings.

Entries should be stories of 1,600–1,800 words and need to be postmarked by 1 March 1998 (note: the closing date has been extended) to **Competition Department (Country Story), Country Origins, PO Box 4, Nairn IV12 4HU.**,

Here are your competition rules:

1. To enter. Entrants must be over 16 years of age at the time of entry and must not have earned an aggregate of more than £10,000 from their writing in the last ten years. Employees of Writers News Limited and regular contributors to magazines published by Writers News Limited are not eligible to enter either competition.

2. Entries should be typed in double spacing on single sides of A4 paper accompanied by a front sheet stating entrant's name, address and phone number and the word count of the story.

3. Entries must be the original material not previously submitted for publication nor currently submitted to any other competition (nor will they be so submitted before the date given in rule 7).

4. Entries will be returned if accompanied by a stamped and addressed envelope. If you wish receipt of your entry to be acknowledged, please enclose a suitably worded stamped and self-addressed postcard. Whilst every care will be taken with manuscripts, the competition organisers cannot be responsible for lost, damaged or delayed material.

5. Entries must be accompanied by a copy of the entry form (see card opposite pages 114-115) together with the entry fee. Entry fee for each competition is £2.50 minimum, £3.50 is the preferred fee, whilst £5 would be welcome to assist with the work of the DT Charitable Trust. All payments should be made to the DT Charitable Trust. Because of high bank charges, overseas currency is not accepted and overseas entrants are therefore advised to send six International Reply Coupons as entry fee.

6. Judging: Competitions will be judged by persons appointed by the agents of the David Thomas Charitable Trust, and the decision of the judges will be final and no correspondence or discussion will be entered into.

7. A first prize of £100 plus a Sharp Font writer will be awarded and the winner will also hold the Country Story Silver Cup for one year. Two runners-up prizes of £100 each will also be awarded. Prizes will be presented at the awards event to be held in London in April 1998 and to which winners will be invited. Winners will be notified by 4 April 1998 and the winning entry will be published in *Writing Magazine*. Entries may be submitted for publication elsewhere after the given notification date.

8. The trustees of the David Thomas Charitable Trust retains the right to publish (in full or abridged) winning and runners-up entries in any book, magazine or publication issues by or associated with Writers News Limited without further payment. Entrants undertake not to make any other use of winning or runners-up entries for eighteen months after the announcement of results without written permission. Copyright remains vested the entrant.

HISTORY IN OUR LANDSCAPE

Mow Cop

HIGH above the Cheshire Plain, but on the borders of Staffordshire, Mow Cop rears up, nearly 1,100 feet above sea level, and is visible for miles around. Originally a mock ruin, built in the 18th century, it has a more unusual reason for its fame, as the birth-place of Primitive Methodism. Hugh Bourne, who was a preacher and wheelwright from Stoke, and William Clowes, who was a champion dancer from Burslem, gathered a group of worshippers, who wanted the simplicity of meeting and worshipping out of doors. Their meeting at Mow Cop, on a Sunday in May 1807, lasted for fourteen hours, and led to similar meetings elsewhere. Hugh Bourne was dismissed as a preacher, and afterwards formed the Primitive Methodist Church, which remained separate until 1932. In 1937, thousands of Methodists came here to worship and celebrate the fact that it was being handed over to the National Trust. - *J Sarsby*

REFLECTIONS

The Great Snow

FIFTY years ago there came the winter of what is still called the Great Snow. There have been other hard winters and wetter winters and longer winters, but nothing to equal the fall of '47. It was especially savage on the hill farms of northern England. Those who battled against the elements for more than eight long weeks will never forget the toil and heartache. One who remembers it all too vividly is Rose Walmsley, who was then living with her husband Fred and two-year old daughter Heather at isolated New House Farm, perched on the 1,000ft contour in Upper Wharfedale:

'I can remember it as if it were yesterday. It hadn't been too bad a winter, and when it got through to February we thought we were over the worst of it. Then it started one Sunday. On the Friday we'd killed a pig and on the Saturday we salted it. On the Sunday, Fred was busy sawing wood, when suddenly the sky clouded over and the snowstorm came out of the north.

It was fine, powdery snow, whizzing round and swirling all over the place. It just kept on snowing and the terrific wind never stopped. By Tuesday the snow had blown level with the roof at the back of the house, forming a tunnel between the building and a huge drift. At the other side you couldn't even see the front door or windows.

I let Fred out of the back bedroom window into the snow tunnel using pig blocks - he was terrified I was going to drop him! He then forced his way round to the front and started to dig down to the outside door, making seven deep steps in the snow.

On the Wednesday things improved a bit and the sun came out. We knew we had to get Heather down to Grassington where she could safely stay with Fred's parents. All we had was a horse and a hay sled, so what we did was to line a dustbin with big hessian sacks. We then put Heather inside, tied the bin to the sled and Fred set off. I shall never forget the sight of this little figure with just her gloves visible as she clung on to the sides.

The snow had blown right over the tops of the gates and walls and it was freezing so hard that it was very crisp. It supported the weight of both the horse and the sled. Fred simply set off in a straightish line and eventually got down to Grassington. There were no tractors or snowploughs, so he picked up some meat and vegetables to leave at the hospital on the way back. They were running short and were right glad to see him. Finally he landed

New House Farm, perched on the 1,000ft contour in Upper Wharfedale. This view dates from the late 1930s.

back; he had to leave the mare in the snow tunnel as there was nowhere else for it.

Soon afterwards it dulled in and started to snow again. It carried on like this for weeks on end, with two or three days of blizzard and then a bit of sunshine before more snow came. But there was never enough sun to start a thaw and so the drifts got higher and higher.

The wind never let up neither. It was what Fred called a lazy wind - it would blow through you rather than round you. It searched out every crack, forcing the snow through the sash windows. There was even a drift in the passageway formed by snow coming through the front door keyhole.

We had ten cows tied up inside the barn and each day it took us hours to muck out. Everything had to be carried by climbing up and over the snow. Then we had to find the trough so that we could bucket water to the cattle. Each night the drifts had blown over it. We also had to feed the horse which was still living inside the snow tunnel.

The biggest job of all was getting fuel inside the house. Fortunately we'd plenty of wood and we heaped the logs right up the chimney so that we had a roaring fire to keep us warm. We kept the boiler in the back kitchen full of water by opening the window and getting shovelfuls of snow, although it's amazing how much we needed.

It's a good thing we'd killed the pig just before the snow started as it meant we were all right for meat.

The pork froze solid in the pantry and kept for weeks on end. We rolled the sides up for bacon and I cooked spare rib in all sorts of different ways. Often I would casserole it slowly in the fireside oven – it smelt wonderful and tasted delicious.

Fred always believed in keeping enough of everything to last a month. We had lots of oats and so had porridge every day. We also had plenty of spuds and were all right for turnips which had been got in to be chopped up for the cows. There was lots of flour in eight-stone bags, so Fred brought back a great block of yeast and I made bread. We also made our own butter and had eggs from our own hens so we didn't do too bad considering.

It was April before the sun at last started to melt the snow and lamb-ing time that year was dreadful. Even then it took ages for it all to go and there was plenty still around in June. Heather was away for eight or nine weeks before we dare bring her back.

We've had other bad winters but nothing like 1947. Today it's very different if it snows hard. Farms have electricity and tractors with a bucket on the front. All we had were oil lamps and hand shovels.

It was a winter I shall never ever forget – I didn't see another woman from February until May.

Rose Walmsley was talking to David Joy

Rose, Heather and Fred Walmsley outside New House Farm about 1950. In the winter of 1947, seven deep steps were cut in the snow at this point in order to get down to the front door.

Modern Military Records

OUR title modern military records looks at the three main military forces we have in the UK today, that of the Army, Navy and Royal Air Force (RAF), and it takes a look at those records which have been created and stored since 1914.

The Army

The British Army including those resident in Wales and Scotland (from 1707) has been in existence since from around Anglo-Saxon times, although the first standing army was not created until 1660. From 1780 to 1914 enlistment was voluntary and usually for life, although few stayed the full term, and was manned by commissioned officers. In 1914 it all started to change, the onset of World War 1 meant that men were required to fight for their country, so enlistment became compulsory once again, until 1960 when National Service (conscription) was abolished.

Records for the Army after 1913 are not held at the Public Record Office (PRO) at Kew, but at the Ministry of Defence records office in Hayes, Middlesex. This repository is not open to the public, but requests can be made in writing. There are many thousands of documents relating to those people employed by The Army and finding them all can give a really good life history of a person who has dedicated their life to the defence of their country.

It is a lot easier to find information on an officer than a normal soldier purely because there are published lists of officers and their careers. The types of records at your disposal (but by no means all) include:

* *The Army Lists.* The first official list was published in 1740 and gives the service history of commissioned officers. From 1754-1879 they were published annually, and from 1879-1900 quarterly. They are arranged by regiment, with a name index from 1766 and from 1879 the list is in order of seniority and includes such details as dates of birth and promotions. Copies can be found at the PRO in WO65 and WO66.

* *Discharge dates and pensions.* Before 1871 there was no general entitlement to a retirement pension. For commissioned officers one of two things could happen, they could be taken off active duty and put on half pay or they could sell their commission. Remember that being pensioned off didn't mean you had come to retirement age, but that your term

of service had come to an end. The Royal Chelsea Hospital also played a significant role taking on the pensions of retired officers. However in 1916 the Ministry of Pensions was created to take over the role of the many different parties involved, but this wasn't a tidy solution with changes taking place all the time. Records of pensions can be a valuable source as they detail not only the amount paid, but the current residence of those being paid. They are organised by district pay office and amongst other details, give the regiment in which the individual served.

* *Regimental Service Records.* These were not universally kept until the 19th century. At this time the War Office became interested in who was employed, where and how they could be deployed in times of crises. This batch of records is still likely to be with the regimental museum or at Hayes. There are some at the PRO but this whole batch is tied to a thirty year closure order.

* *Regimental Registers of Birth 1761-1924.* These are held at St Catherine's House. They are indexed and gives the regiment and place of birth of children born to the wives of serving officers.

* *Muster Books and Pay Lists.* Are organised by year in date order. They can give information such as age, place of enlistment and trade. From 1868 to 1883 they also include marriage rolls, which can give information about wives and children.

* *Casualty Returns.* As well as listing casualties they also include absences, desertions and surcharges as well as the wounded or dead. They are usually organised by regiment and in monthly or quarterly returns. They can give such information as name, rank, place of birth, trade on

enlistment, date, place and nature of casualty, any debts or credits and next of kin.

* *Medical Records.* When a soldier was injured at war his movements were tracked each step of the way. Every treatment point would log into an Admission Book the name, initials, rank, number, regiment, and date of admission together with a brief description. Operation log books would record each patient who had been operated on. Case cards would be kept at the bottom of the bed and one in the office. During the World War 1 around 2.5 million were created in total. At the end of the war they came together and were spilt for statistical purposes and all 26 tons then ended up with the Ministry of Health and Pensions. By 1975 all those liable to claim a pension were now on old age pension, so nearly the whole lot were destroyed.

From World War 2 onwards finding information on those who died is a lot easier than those still living, as most of the records have closure orders on them. The PRO holds an Army Roll of Honour 1939-1945 in WO304 which lists those men and women who died. There are also the War Office Weekly Casualty lists which started on 7 August 1917 and copies can be found in the British Newspaper Library. Other sources include; eighty volumes of Soldiers in the Great War, found in many libraries and on microfilm; local newspapers reported deaths and casualties usually with a photo; the Absent Voters List which allowed service men to register to obtain a vote in their own constituency;

Service Medals or Award Rolls; and Court Martial.

The Navy

During the middle ages the Navy was managed by the King in Council. After 1302 this was transferred to an official known as the Lord or High Admiral. He generally commanded in person and was responsible for policy, strategy and fighting personnel. He also had legal functions being the President of the High Court of Admiralty. From 1546 the administration of the Navy was carried out by a group of officers appointed by letters patent and later became known as the Navy Board. From 1708 after the position had been left vacant many times, the High Admiral's responsibilities were taken over by the Board of Admiralty.

After 1660 officers and men had to make oaths of allegiance to the Kings and these records can be found at the PRO. At the end of the Napoleonic wars in 1815 the Navy shrank from 145,000 to 19,000 men. At this time there were no means of pensioning off so a survey amongst officers was carried out to see who had the best claim to keep their job. There was no continuous service for ratings until 1853.

As well as the PRO you will find information on the Navy can be found at the Royal Maritime Museum, Royal Naval Museum and museum ships like HMS Victory and Belfast.

Although in this article we have concentrated on those types of records you can access to find out about ancestors in the Navy, the same sorts of records also apply to the allied forces such as the Royal Naval

Reserve established in 1859; the Royal Marines (soldiers of the sea) and the Royal Naval Air Service founded in 1914 but later amalgamated with the Royal Flying Corps to become the Royal Air Force.

Personnel Records

Service records for those employed by the Navy come in many different forms and by using the various types you should be able to build up a good naval career and history of an individual. The types of records available include:

* *Officers Service Registers.* During the 19th century the Admiralty developed a system of keeping records. These were used to record the officer's career, and in most cases provide a complete career history from enlistment to retirement or death. Few registers prior to 1840 still exist. There are indexes to them and they are on open shelves in the reference room at the PRO. Some of the later editions are subject to extended closure rules.

* *Lieutenants' Passing Certificates.* These were required when an individual was being promoted to a lieutenant. They are summaries of an officer's previous career and training and sometimes include birth or baptism certificates.

* *The Navy List.* This is the official list produced by the Navy of all their officers and identifies which ships they were on. From 1814 it has been published quarterly and gives seniority lists. There were confidential editions produced during the two world war years.

* *Certificate of Service.* These were compiled by the Navy Pay Office usually from the ships' pay books or full and half pay registers. They give the services of warrant officers and ratings who were applying for superannuation or admission to Greenwich Hospital.

* *Commission and Warrants 1695-1849.* They provide successive appointments of officers in chronological order to different ships. There is a card index for some of them.

* *Succession Books.* A form of service record arranged by ship, although most are indexed. They can be used to trace a commissioned or warrant officer. Usually they are organised a page per ship and list the appointments to each position.

* *Leave Books.* These were kept to record the amount of leave granted to an officer.

* *Medal Rolls.* Arranged by ship and then usually by rank and name. They give very little information prior to 1914. They record the names of officers and men who were awarded or claimed medals or slaps issued for gallantry or service in particular campaigns or actions. The set at the PRO is on microfilm and covers the period 1793-1966.

* *Musters and Pay Books.* Were kept by the officer in charge of each ship and recorded when all individuals came on board, their rank, a brief description and background to them, what activities they carried out, what pay they were entitled to and what allowances had been received and therefore had to be deducted from their pay.

There are many types of record available – in fact you could probably spend your whole life looking through them to find out what you need. Some of the other types of records to look out for include: those relating to the two world wars; war diaries; black books; logs and journals; prisoners of war; pensions and court martial.

Royal Air Force

The Royal Air Force was not formed until 1 April 1918. Prior to this our air defence was the responsibility of the Army's Royal Flying Corps (1912) and the Navy's Royal Naval Air Service (1914). Because very few records giving details of individuals are available for public inspection, due to thirty or 75 year closure orders on them, what is covered here will primarily deal with those who did not make it back from the various war efforts. You can however, get details of a direct ancestor by writing to the Personnel Sections of RAF Barnwood or RAF Innsworth.

The only really complete listing of personnel which exists is the 1918 Muster List which was generated on its formation, and is in alphabetical order. There is also a regular publication which gives the career of an officer called the Air Force List, it does not show where an officer is serving.

When the RAF was formed in 1918, four gallantry awards were introduced. The medal rolls do not give detailed information, merely their name and regimental/service number. They are usually arranged by regiment/battalion, then by rank and name. There are no indexes. The medal roll for World War 1 is on microfiche and includes RAF personnel amongst them.

Swearing Johnny

In the days before frequent travel, traditions varied sharply between places surprisingly close together. Take the question of swearing. In a market town the language was routinely blue; at a cove on the coast only a dozen miles away it was the King's English.

'Bugger you, don't give me that damn you, I never swear,' said a bus driver in all seriousness, defending himself against a charge that he was using bad language in front of ladies. Only the Swearing Johnny really shocked. A gentle enough worker at most times, occasionally he would climb the church roof and shout in language that was said to upset even the dogs.

Yet at the cove, the boatmen were seriously shocked when 'up country' visiting gentry used bad language while catching mackerel. For that matter they were upset when these superior visitors attempted to bargain the price of an hour's mackerel fishing, or of a lobster caught earlier, for the tradition here was that the price you asked was to be taken or left.

Needless to say, one day, for a reason nobody fathomed, the Swearing Johnny visited the cove. Coming over peculiar, and there being no church tower instantly to hand, he rowed himself to the middle of the bay and shouted obscenities until the police arrived.

REFLECTIONS

Life as a Land Girl

Working as a team

TODAY one man ploughs his furrow alone, or drives comfortably in the rain, with a cab to protect him and a radio to entertain him.

During World War 2, land girls were more likely to be ploughing a team of three, exposed to wind and rain on a Fordson tractor without a cab. No Radio Sussex to sing them along or give them a time check. But perhaps they were closer to the land that way, conscious of each furrow ploughed and the gulls wheeling overhead, unmolested by the squall of pop music.

It was all team work then, with a laugh and a joke or a grumble and groan. From the time the corn was cut, a team of men followed the binder to stook the sheaves. Later a team of men built them into ricks, and in the winter it was threshed and sold. Fields had a different look in those days, with the corn shocks and ricks on the skyline. Now a combine harvester sweeps the land bare, with only one man to operate it, leaving just the high stubble, the whole operation done at one go.

Now the machine has taken over, and the farm labourer scarcely exists except as a mechanic. Then, it was good to take a break and talk over a flask of tea in the fields. Simple basic conversation, but the farm labourer had his own droll sense of humour, and the work went merrier for a brief exchange of words.

In the dairy, milking machines were introduced during the war, but mucking out remained arduous, with buckets of water fetched from the yard and a stout broom to scrub the brickwork. Now the milking parlour dispenses with all that and the milk flows through a glass tube into the dairy. No labouring with four gallon buckets of milk to be carried up the steps and tipped into the cooler at shoulder level. The cowman has merely to monitor the procedure, and even the feed can be mechanically distributed.

On the farm where the author was a landgirl, cow sheds and stables now stand empty and derelict. Formerly there were sheep, pigs, cows and horses, but now it is totally arable and there is no stock of any kind.

The memory remains of the group of men standing at the farm entrance at 7 am, bikes propped up against the fence. Time to roll a fag. What they said didn't amount to much, but it was a good way to start the day, and the foreman would tell them where they were to work before they dispersed.

Today's tractor driver misses out - for him, no early morning chats, no shared tea breaks and no gossip.

Morning Milking

THERE is an enduring image of light at quarter to five in the morning, and it always seemed to be winter. The stove dead in the kitchen. Ash fluffed out between the bars. The flask of tea on the table, made the night before. Not particularly hot. No words spoken.

The meadow stiff with frost as we walk down to the farm. A clatter of wings as a pheasant starts up.

In the dairy the clash of buckets, a noisy oath, the rattle of chains as the cows crowd into the yard and go to their places, heads lowered, wary. Hooves slip on greasy tiles. Sometimes a newcome heifer gets it wrong and wedges herself between two others. 'I'll 'elp you!' shouts the under cowman.

Once settled there is a steady sound of contentment as they munch the sweet hay and cattlecake, broken by the clatter of bucket and stool or the spatter of urine in the gutter. The doors are closed and it begins to feel warm. Lit by hurricane lamps the place is full of shadows, the air thick with the smell of stale milk, paraffin and dung.

Tom, the head cowman, has come without his teeth, which is a bad sign. He has a sardonic view of life. Lean and hollow-cheeked he looks old at thirty. The under cowman was in the navy and is nicknamed The Fleet.

We put on our milking smocks in silence. It's a comfort to lean against the warm flank of a cow as milking gets under way. This and the rhythmic movement of the hands makes for drowsiness. Breakfast seems far away. Ten more cows to go.

Derelict barn at Langford Fam, Lavant

The author, Brenda Lismer, in her land girl days, with a farmhand

At five to seven Tom opens the end door facing the farm gate where the field workers are gathered for a smoke and a gossip before starting work. One of them breaks away and comes through the door, swinging his milk can. He brings a note of cheerfulness from the outside world.

Milking is finished. Smocks removed. Boots brushed with the broom. The churns are heaved on to the platform for the lorry to collect.

Home to breakfast before the hard work of mucking out begins.

The One That Got Away

THE D-Day traffic passed along the Midhurst road day and night in a continuous stream, routed through the farm where the land girl was working.

She had the unwelcome task of driving the cows across this road from one meadow to another. It was a tricky operation as tanks and lorries were on the move in a never ending line. There should have been someone with her to hold up the traffic, but the cowmen had gone home to breakfast.

It was now or never when a short gap finally appeared in the formidable procession, and she desperately opened the gate. With prayer in her heart she held up a hand to the oncoming lorry, but in a strange situation cows are silly, and one of them dodged out to assault the vehicle. Taken by surprise, it came to a screeching halt.

The land girl felt as though she was holding up the whole of the war as the herd, now mobile, jostled in a close pack to the meadow opposite where the grass was sweeter, but she had to see the job through, feeling small and ordinary in a routine that couldn't stop for Hitler.

Meanwhile the lorry driver who had come to such an abrupt halt, had climbed down from the cab to inspect his vehicle.

'The big end's gorn,' he announced gloomily and the land girl's guilt deepened.

It was fortunate that there was a REME encampment on the farm to deal with such emergencies. He was able to make a U turn in the meadow and the invasion continued without him. – *Brenda Lismer*

Overleaf: The author, Brenda Lismer, in land girl days

Questions and Answers

Do you need help, advice, others to work with? Then this section is for you. To have your question answered in the magazine on this page, send your question to Questions and Answers, *Country Origins*, Inverwick House, Albert Street, Nairn IV12 4HE.

In this picture is a metal item with a wooden handle which I came across in my grandmother's closet. It appears to be an item for the garden and is about 26 inches long, but I have no idea what it would have been used for. Do you have any idea?
From information we have found it would appear that this is in fact a carpet stretcher. It dates from around the 1900s and the handle is likely to be made of birch.

Committee boards of directors of a company and even political parties have a Chairman who is the one in charge of the meeting and keeps control and order. Do you have any idea where this word might have come from or why this term is used in these instances?
The term chairman in fact dates from Medieval times. The Lord of the Manor when sitting at the high table would have a chair – he would control others in the room and they would not eat until he was seated, served and started first. He would usually be the only one in the room with this privilege while others would sit on stools or on the floor. In fact it was considered such a status symbol of the time that he would even take it away with him when on trips visiting others.

When delving through family history books to find out where and what information can be accessed and used for my research, I keep coming across the term Chapman County Codes. Can you help me by letting me know what these might be ?
The Chapman County Codes are an abbreviated set of codes devised by Colin Chapman to allow each of the counties to be abbreviated when used in text books or when you are writing them down. The majority of them are three letter codes and conform to the British Standards Institute set BSI6879:1987. An example of such codes include BDF for Bedfordshire;

WIL for Wiltshire and BRK for Berkshire. When doing your research if you can use these codes you will find transcribing a lot quicker, and the more you use them the more natural it becomes, but in the early days be aware that errors could occur as some of the codes are similar.

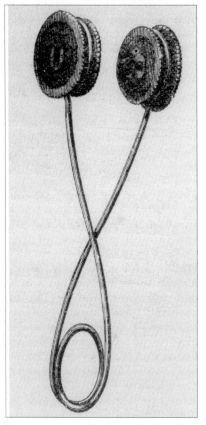

I came across the item in the photograph amongst a box of miscellaneous items I picked up at a car boot sale. Do you have any idea what they might be? They look remarkably like a pair of food handlers.

This item is a tourmaline pincette and it was used by students to see the effects of light through crystals. A slice of tourmaline would be mounted so as to be capable of rotation at each end of the spring tongs, and the crystal plate to be examined would be held between them. The rays would pass through into the small pupil of the eye and converge sufficiently to show the effect.

An ancestor of mine emigrated to Australia around the beginning of the early 1800s, and took with him his wife and two children at the time. I believe they had further children once they were settled there. Are there any records within this country that I can access to find out when and where they may have settled?
There was a census produced for New South Wales and Tasmania in 1828 and it contains some 35,000 persons and their ages, religions, land held and so on. It also indicates whether they went to the colony free or in bond or whether they were born there, together with the ship and year of arrival. A copy of this census is on microfilm and is held at the Public Record Office at Kew in HO10/21-27.

I had the tv on the other day listening to a gardening programme but my mind was on other things. They were looking at older methods of gardening and how gardeners of the past coped with some of the problems of the day. They mentioned something about a 'knocking

stick' but I didn't get back to the tv in time to find out what it was. This has been puzzling me for a while now, do you have any idea what they might have been referring to?

A knocking stick was in simple terms a piece of bent wood looking a bit like a hammer. You would hold the straight end and tap the bent end against a flower pot and listen for the noise. If a dull noise was omitted then it did not require watering. On the other hand if a ringing sound was heard then the plant needed water to survive. Try it yourself, you'll be surprised!

Where can I access details of a death certificate without having to make the trip to St Catherine's House in London? I am not as mobile as I used to be and would find a trip to London exhausting.

Death certificate details can be obtained through the post but first you will need to identify the St Catherine's House codes to be able to place your order. Unfortunately you did not mention where you came from so we are not able to be specific, but there are various options. You can look at the registers on microfilm at your local Mormon family history centre or local larger county library, or you could go to the local registry office where the death was first registered and ask for a copy from them. It is usually cheaper to get the copy from the local office than through St Catherine's, but you will have to determine which is the ideal for you. If you wish to use the postal service of St Catherine's then you need to write

to General Registry Office, Smedley Hydro, Trafalgar Road, Southport PR8 2HH.

I am in the process of restoring an old water pump (around 150 years old), however I have hit a problem. It has an internal lead pipe with an internal bore of 3.5 inch diameter, but the piston and valve have rotted away over the years and I am not sure what the exact length and shape of the valve should be. Do you have any assistance you could give me in this matter?

You can see the problem this reader is having. If any of our readers have either restored such a water pump in the past or have any knowledge or experience that they could pass on to him, could you please drop us a line and we will forward on anything that you are able to help with. The picture is of a water pump, but it is not the one being restored.

Then and Now

The patchwork of styles that make up our villages and towns has continued to develop from the earliest times, adding new styles, the strongest remaining as time goes by. It may be that the new building being put up today will eventually merge in to become part of the patchwork of history represented.

The photographs show views in Strathmiglo, Fife, and were supplied by John Cameron of Dalgety Bay, Fife. The first photograph was taken in 1895, while the second similar view was in 1900. The clock was changed in 1897, the same year as Cadburys produced their first Milk Chocolate, advertised in the window in the later shot, while the earlier one advertises Cadburys Cocoa, and shop fronts on the right have been changed. Next, we have a similar view today. Then we have two views from the opposite side of the clock tower, again representing first 1895 and then 1900. Finally, we have the same view today.

Strathmiglo was the headquarters of Hogg's Fife footwear, who were well known by country people throughout the UK as one of the first pioneers of mail order. Their warehouse was next to the town clock. The town was also known for its linen manufacture which lasted until the 1950s or 60s. The chimney of Thompson's linen factory (not shown) stood around twice the height of other buildings in 1895, but today the site is partly occupied by houses and partly by a joiner's workshop.

The Ashen Faggot

IT was a lot of work for the farm hosting the Boxing Day shoot. Not only was the rabbiting expected to be good, and the lunch even better, but tradition expected the hosts to throw a festive party in the evening – the event of the year for many in the small community centred around the west Devon village of Bratton Clovelly.

As soon as the day's sport was over, everyone rushed home to see to the milking, feed the stock and change for the party. By 7 o'clock entire families, lanterns to hand and dressed in Sunday best, would be heading across ink-dark fields to the farmhouse. Cars were scarce in 1930s rural Devon and anyway, walking to and from the party was much more fun.

The ground floor of the house was usually cleared of furniture to make room for an evening of dance, story telling and song. There was always an accordion player, a fiddler or two and someone with a set of bones, that fistful of dried pigs ribs played like the spoons and of which the village boasted several virtuosos.

The centre-piece of most rooms was the open hearth. Some were up to 8ft wide and lined with cloam ovens used daily for baking and breadmaking. Hanging from the chimney throat were the black iron crooks on which hung the hot water fountain and the cooking pots. In the centre of the hearth, pushed up against the charcoal coated back-stick, the fire sizzled away. Three or four iron pokers, ready for mulling jugs of cider, rested in the hot ashes.

Laughter, music and dance

ACCORDING to tradition, specially prepared 'ashen faggots' were always burnt at the Boxing Day party. Ash poles, about one inch thick and 3 to 4ft in length, were gathered into bundles, or faggots, some 18ins across and bound tightly with as many as a dozen split willow or hazel wands. With great ceremony each faggot would be placed on the fire. As successive bindings burnt through with a sharp crack and a shower of sparks, the adults, encouraged by tradition and the rising temperature, took another glass of mulled or spiced cider. By the third faggot, the party was usually going well.

As the dancers found their feet and the reels came faster, so jackets came off and the sound of boots, clacking on the flagstone floor to the rhythm of home grown music, grew louder. For the next few hours the partygoers would be lost to a world of laughter, music and dance. The reality of the sobering walk home through the cold night air and the chore of early morning milking would come soon enough. – *Bernard Cole*

Sketching and Painting Nature

Special Weekend Break in the Peak District National Park Losehill Hall

Friday 12th to Sunday 14th December 1997
All inclusive price £130

Losehill Hall, the Peak District National Park Centre is offering an outstanding opportunity to spend a winter weekend later this year amid the magnificent scenery of the Peak District National Park in the company of Frederick J. Watson, an internationally respected wildlife artist (otherwise known as Derick). An informal approach, plenty of encouragement and evening demonstrations will inspire you with all the confidence you need.

As well as a packed programme and the chance to practise and perfect your artistic skills, you will be treated to sherry and mince pies on arrival, and a full Christmas dinner on Sunday night. The price of £130 includes all tuition, accommodation, meals and transport during the weekend.

Where You will be Staying
Losehill Hall is a converted Victorian manor house set in beautiful landscape grounds, the Hall is run by the Peak district National Park Authority, so choosing a holiday at Losehill really is a unique way to experience the special qualities of the National Park.

All the accommodation is en-suite, in single or twin rooms, with a choice of menus at each meal, including a vegetarian option. Losehill Hall can also cater for special diets including dairy free, low fat etc. Meals include a full English or continental breakfast, large packed lunches and generous four course dinners. Tea, coffee and biscuits are provided during the day and they also have a guests' kitchen for those late night cuppas.

Losehill Hall is situated about ten minutes walk from the pretty village of Castleton, with its numerous pubs and gift shops. For those who prefer to spend a cosy evening by the fire, Losehill Hall also has its own licensed bar, stocking a wide range of speciality beers and whiskies. There's also a shop for those last minute essentials and souvenirs of your stay.

Send for your Booking form to:
Sue Field/Jane Warren
Losehill Hall
Peak National Park Centre
Castleton
Derbyshire, S30 2WB
Tel: 01433 620373
Fax 01433 620346

Collectors Corner

Musical memories on 78s

THE village of Foxton, a few miles southwest of Cambridge, is home to the largest supplier of 78 rpm gramophone records in Europe. Specialising in the popular music of the past, 'Greg's Greats' provides musical memories of happy days to hundreds of nostalgia seekers and record collectors throughout the world.

From Al Jolson to Elvis Presley, from Music Hall to Rock and Roll, the stock of over 60,000 discs covers all musical genres from 1900 to 1960.

Catalogues covering 50s Pop, Jazz, Rock 'n' Roll, Blues, Skiffle, C&W, Boogie & Gospel are available on request. Those looking for dance bands, musical comedy, film stars or vocals from an earlier age are invited to send in their 'request' list or to phone to arrange a personal visit to browse through the records at leisure.

Greg can be contacted on 01223 872 937 by phone or fax.

Popular publications

YESTERDAY'S NEWS really began when proprietor Ed Jones was a child and became an avid collector and reader of newspapers, magazines and comics. Friends and relatives would also contribute their old copies and nothing was ever thrown away.

'We began the business of marketing the newspapers in 1967. We invite people to present newspapers and magazines of the day or week of their friends' and relatives' birthdays. People do buy older ones as well and the most sought after subject is the sinking of the Titanic on April 15th, 1912, closely followed by the reports on Jack the Ripper and then third in popularity is the winning of the World Cup in 1966.

'We have 100,000 newspapers and magazines in eight rooms,' adds Ed, 'even though it's only a semi-detached. It's lucky we have a basement!'

History of heroes

MEDAL NEWS is the world's only independent magazine devoted to medals, battles and the history of heroes. Covering mainly British and Commonwealth medals and heroes, *Medal News* (£2.50) regularly features stories of gallantry, life-saving and heroism across the ages as well as articles, auction reports, news, views and readers' queries.

Lost medals can be traced through the 'Medal Tracker' service and classified advertisements, both of which are free to subscribers.

To complement the magazine, Token Publishing Ltd also publishes the *Medal Yearbook* (ISBN 1870 192 141, 336pp, £12.95). An annual, fully illustrated price guide and aid to collectors. This year's edition includes a new photographic medal ribbon chart, a commonwealth medal section, a guide to last year's auctions and a complete index to *Medal News*.